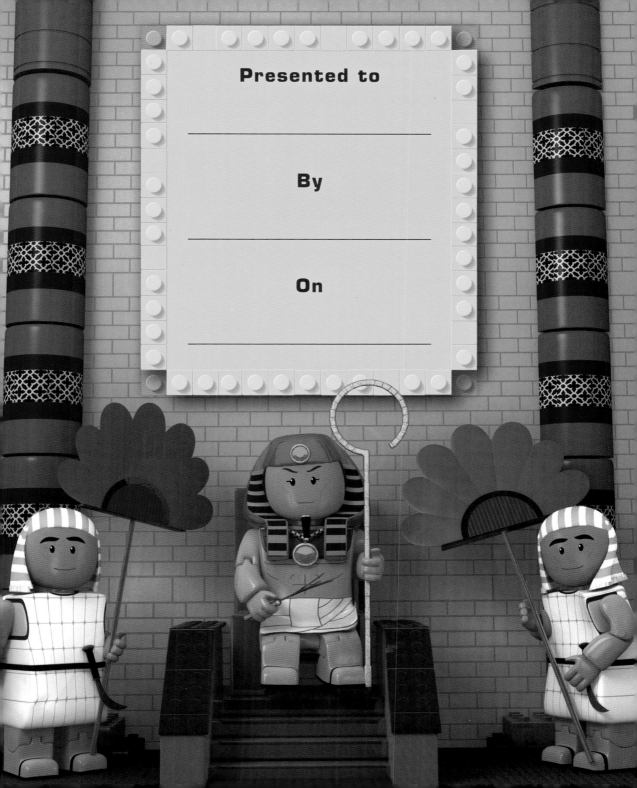

Presented to

_____

By

_____

On

_____

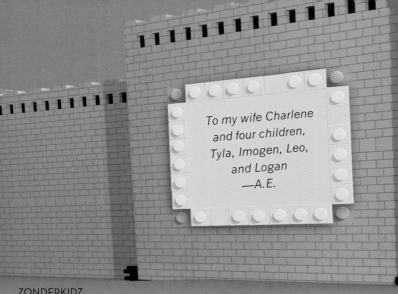

To my wife Charlene
and four children,
Tyla, Imogen, Leo,
and Logan
—A.E.

ZONDERKIDZ

Brick Builders Illustrated Bible
Copyright © 2018 by Zondervan
Illustrations © 2018 by Zondervan

This title is also available as a Zondervan ebook. Visit www.zondervan.com/ebooks.

Requests for information should be addressed to:
Zonderkidz, 3900 *Sparks Dr. SE,* Grand Rapids, Michigan 49546

ISBN 978-0-310-75437-4

Library of Congress Cataloging-in-Publication Data

Names: Dammer, Emily, author.
Title: Brick builder's illustrated Bible / by Emily Dammer.
Description: Grand Rapids : Zonderkidz, 2018. | Series: Brick builders storybook Bible
Identifiers: LCCN 2018029027| ISBN 9780310754374 (hardcover) | ISBN 9780310754503
Subjects: LCSH: Bible stories, English.
Classification: LCC BS551.3 .D36 2018 | DDC 220.95/05--dc23 LC record available at https://lccn.loc.gov/2018029027

Content Contributor: Emily Dammer
Editor: Barbara Herndon
Art direction and design: Jody Langley
Printed in China

18 19 20 21 22 23 /DCI/ 22 21 20 19 18 17 16 15 14 13 12 11 10 9 8 7 6 5 4 3 2

Encourage one
another with the
hope you have.
Build each other up.
In fact, that's what
you are doing.

1 THESSALONIANS 5:11

BRICK BUILDERS
ILLUSTRATED BIBLE

OVER 35 BIBLE STORIES FOR KIDS

Illustrated by Antony Evans

Written by Emily Dammer

ZONDER**kidz**

Table of Contents

OLD TESTAMENT

NEW TESTAMENT

8

God's Colorful Creation

Genesis 1–2

In the beginning, there was nothing but darkness—
no yellow, no green, and no blue.

So God decided to build the earth. He used so
many different, exciting colors like orange, red, and
purple.

On the first day of creation, God called out, "Let
there be light!" And yellow light appeared above
the earth. God called it "day." When the light
disappeared, God called the darkness "night."

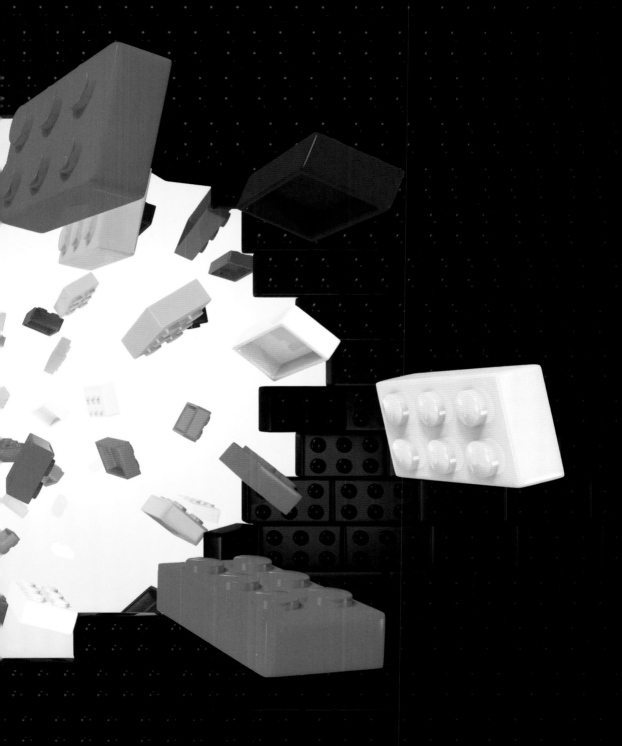

11

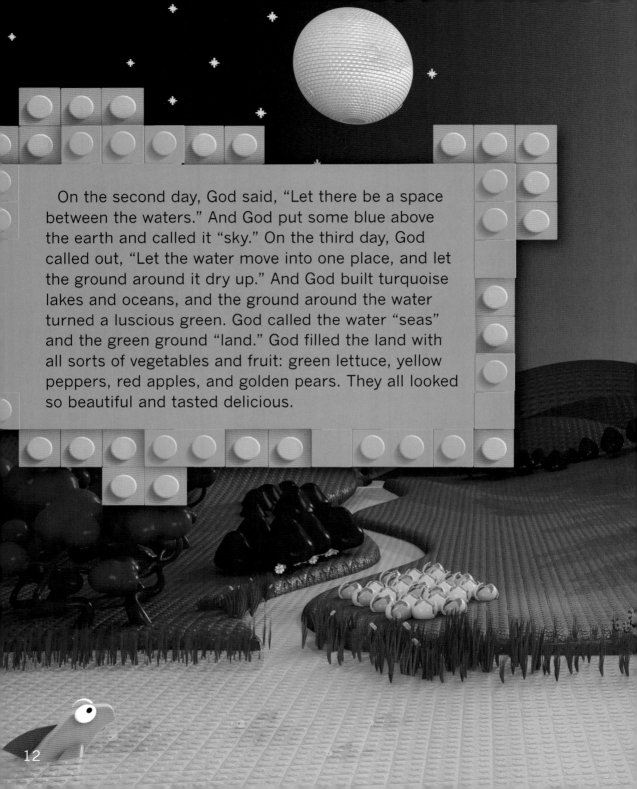

On the second day, God said, "Let there be a space between the waters." And God put some blue above the earth and called it "sky." On the third day, God called out, "Let the water move into one place, and let the ground around it dry up." And God built turquoise lakes and oceans, and the ground around the water turned a luscious green. God called the water "seas" and the green ground "land." God filled the land with all sorts of vegetables and fruit: green lettuce, yellow peppers, red apples, and golden pears. They all looked so beautiful and tasted delicious.

"Let there be a golden sun and grey moon in the sky," God said on the fourth day. And then he added twinkling, yellow stars.

On the fifth day, God said, "Let there be birds in the sky and fish in the sea." And God designed them in every color.

13

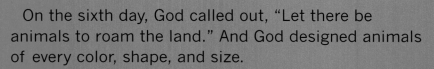

On the sixth day, God called out, "Let there be animals to roam the land." And God designed animals of every color, shape, and size.

Everything was so beautiful and so wonderfully built, but there was something missing. God wanted to build something that could enjoy all that he had created.

So on the same day he designed the animals to roam the land, God designed people in his own image. He built Adam and Eve. And they were beautiful and wonderful too.

On the seventh day, God looked over all of his designs and called out, "What a magnificent creation!" And he rested, delighted with what he had built.

14

BUILDING BLOCK

Praise him!
Praise God for all of
his beautiful creation.
Thank him for what he
built just for us.

15

The Juicy Red Fruit

Genesis 3

In the Garden of Eden there were two beautiful tall trees. One tree was called the Tree of Life, and the other was called the Tree of Knowledge of Good and Evil.

God told Adam and Eve they could enjoy everything and eat anything in the garden except the juicy red fruit that grew from the Tree of Knowledge. But Eve did not listen to God.

One day, Eve was admiring the Tree of Knowledge, watching the leaves blow back and forth when suddenly, a snake slithered out. "Eve!" the snake hissed. "Did God really say you couldn't eat from this tree?"

"God told us we could eat any food in this garden!" answered Eve. "But, we are not allowed to eat the fruit from this tree. If we eat the fruit, we will die!"

The sneaky snake laughed. "Oh, Eve, you won't die if you eat this fruit." He pulled a bright red fruit from one of the branches. "If you eat this, you will be like God. You will learn what is good and what is evil." Eve took the fruit from the snake and took a huge bite. It was delicious! So Eve called out to Adam, "Try this fruit." Adam took a bite of the fruit and smiled. He agreed. The fruit was delicious.

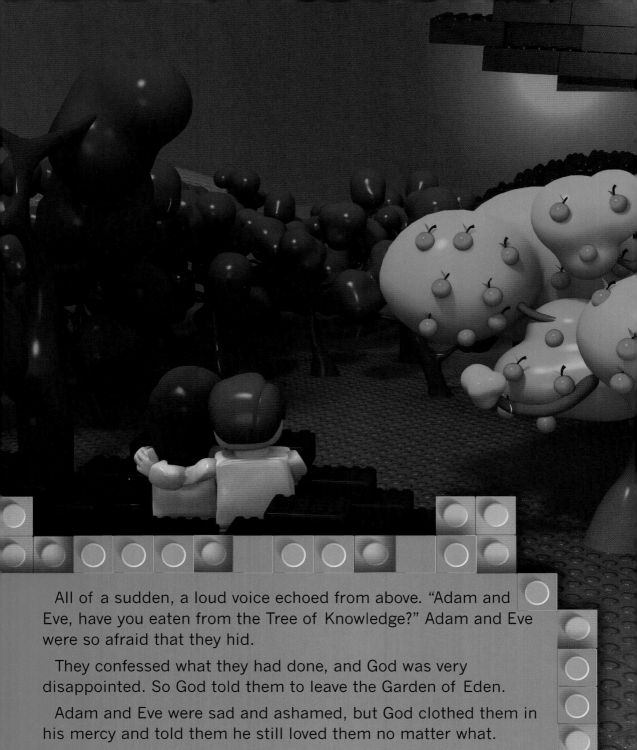

All of a sudden, a loud voice echoed from above. "Adam and Eve, have you eaten from the Tree of Knowledge?" Adam and Eve were so afraid that they hid.

They confessed what they had done, and God was very disappointed. So God told them to leave the Garden of Eden.

Adam and Eve were sad and ashamed, but God clothed them in his mercy and told them he still loved them no matter what.

BUILDING BLOCK

Obey God!
Try hard to obey God. But even if you make a mistake, don't worry. God will love you no matter what.

21

The Multicolored Rainbow

Genesis 6–9

A blackness spread across the earth, and God was not happy. He had built creation for people to enjoy, but men and women were behaving badly and sinning.

So God decided to send a flood to destroy the world and everyone in it. Everyone except Noah. God knew that Noah still had a good heart.

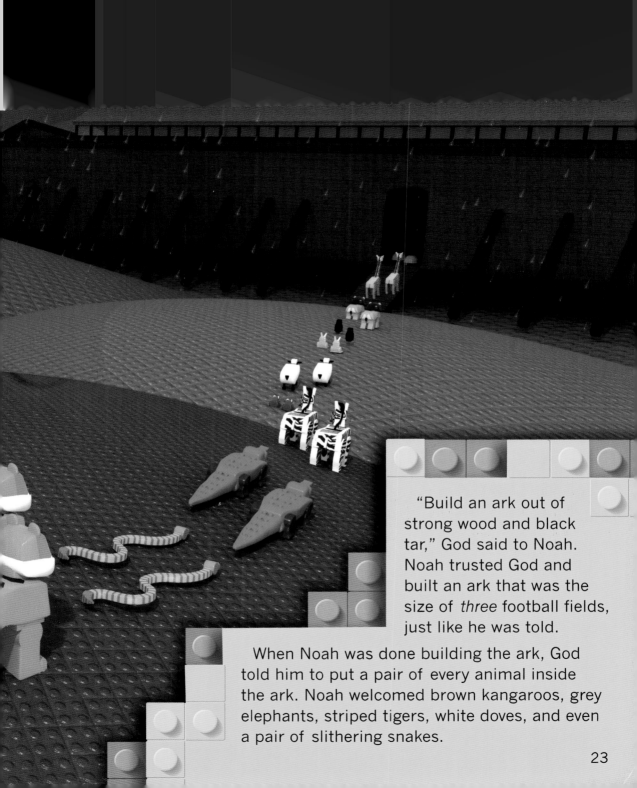

"Build an ark out of strong wood and black tar," God said to Noah. Noah trusted God and built an ark that was the size of *three* football fields, just like he was told.

When Noah was done building the ark, God told him to put a pair of every animal inside the ark. Noah welcomed brown kangaroos, grey elephants, striped tigers, white doves, and even a pair of slithering snakes.

23

Then God told Noah and his family to enter the ark. Noah stepped inside and looked back once more at the green grass that would soon be covered by a flood. God shut Noah and his family inside the ark as rain began pouring down over the earth.

The rain lasted 40 days and 40 nights. But God kept Noah, his family, and all the animals safe inside the ark.

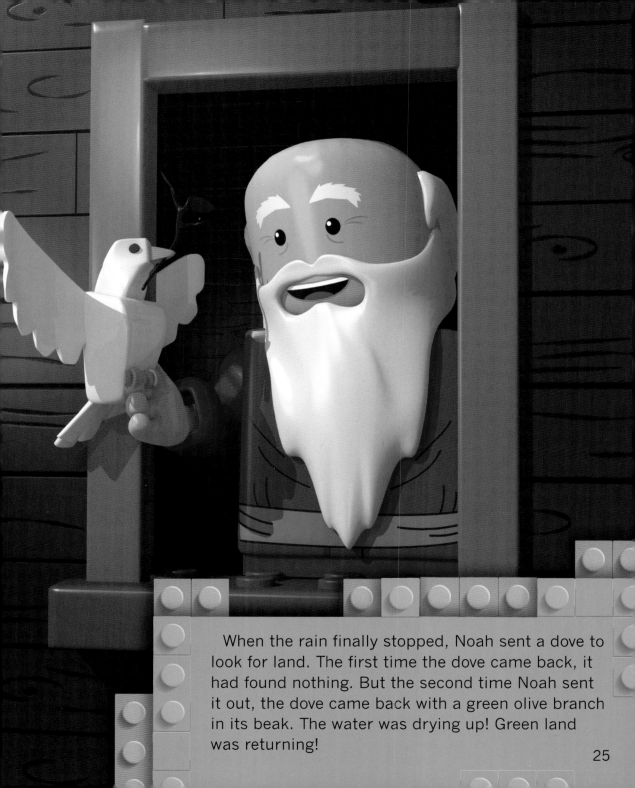

When the rain finally stopped, Noah sent a dove to look for land. The first time the dove came back, it had found nothing. But the second time Noah sent it out, the dove came back with a green olive branch in its beak. The water was drying up! Green land was returning!

25

Noah and his family were happy, and so was God! He even built a magnificent, multicolored rainbow across the sky. It was a sign from God that promised he would never again send a flood to destroy the earth.

BUILDING BLOCK

Trust God!
Noah trusted God so much that he built a huge ark even though people laughed at him. Don't worry even when things get tough. God will always know what is best.

Building the Tower

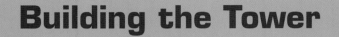

Genesis 11

After the flood, the world filled with people again and they all spoke one language. One day some people decided to build a magnificent city with the tallest tower that ever existed. They wanted others to be jealous of what they could build.

"It will be the prettiest tower ever, with winding stairs and lovely balconies," someone said.

"Yes! And it will have the strongest walls, so no one will be able to get inside unless we let them."

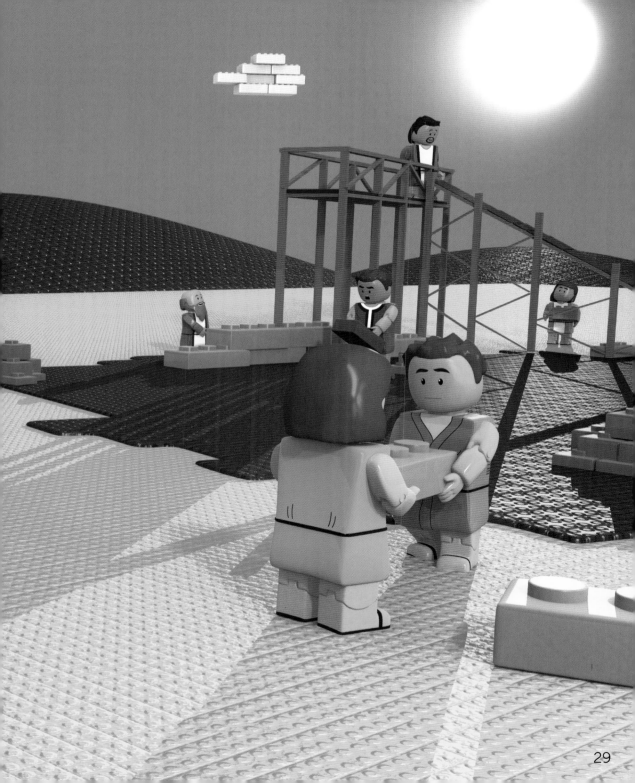

Every day, the men and women would wake up early and add new bricks and cement to make the walls extra strong. Over time, the tower grew taller and taller until it was close to touching the puffy white clouds in the sky.

This worried God. *If they can build such a tall tower speaking the same language, then nothing is impossible for them*, he thought. *They will try to live without my help, and that is not a good way to live.*

So God decided to mix things up by creating new languages. All of a sudden, the people became very confused. They no longer spoke the same language. Then God decided to move the people all over the world, so they couldn't build things without his help.

The tower that was going to reach all the way to heaven became known as the Tower of Babel, because when God mixed up the people's languages, they began to babel.

BUILDING

BLOCK

Serve the Lord!
It's amazing that the whole world only spoke one language. But the people forgot about God and thought only about themselves and their glory. Try to always serve the Lord. Put him first no matter what. He wants to help you with the big and the little things in life.

Abram Trusts God

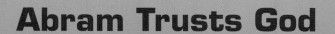

Genesis 15

One night, God came to a man named Abram and told him, "Do not be scared. I will protect you and reward you greatly."

But Abram was afraid. He had no children and he was very old. He asked God, "Lord, what can you give me?" Abram wanted to know how his family would go on after he was gone.

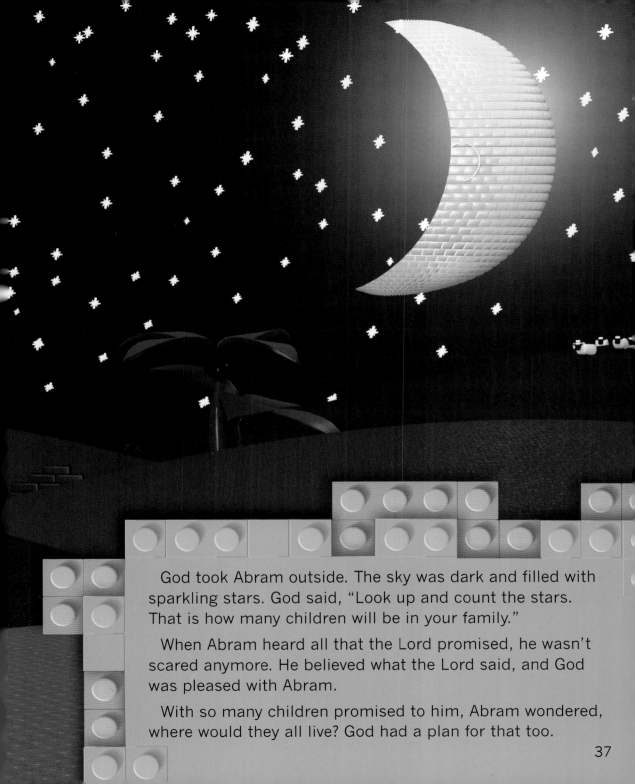

God took Abram outside. The sky was dark and filled with sparkling stars. God said, "Look up and count the stars. That is how many children will be in your family."

When Abram heard all that the Lord promised, he wasn't scared anymore. He believed what the Lord said, and God was pleased with Abram.

With so many children promised to him, Abram wondered, where would they all live? God had a plan for that too.

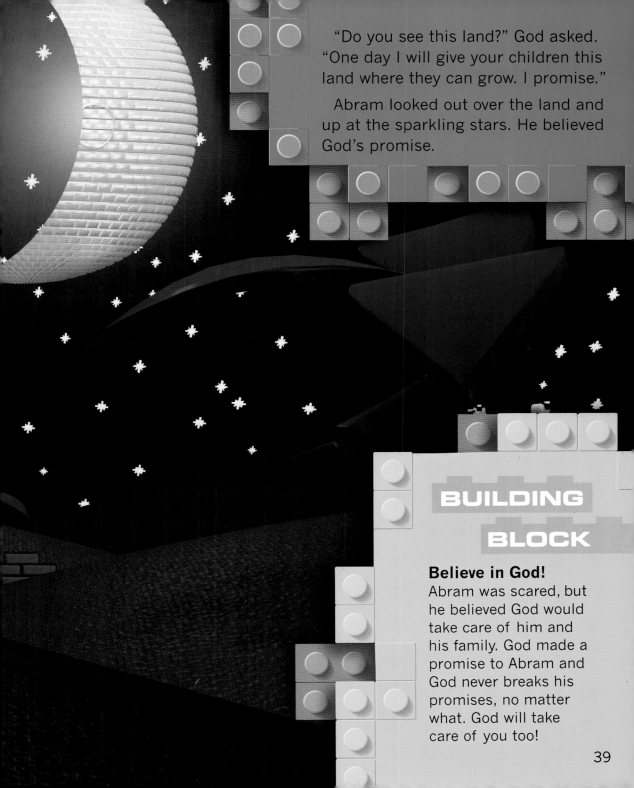

"Do you see this land?" God asked. "One day I will give your children this land where they can grow. I promise."

Abram looked out over the land and up at the sparkling stars. He believed God's promise.

BUILDING BLOCK

Believe in God!
Abram was scared, but he believed God would take care of him and his family. God made a promise to Abram and God never breaks his promises, no matter what. God will take care of you too!

39

Moses and the Red Sea

Exodus 2–14

In Egypt, long after Abram was dead, there lived an evil pharaoh. He ordered all the Hebrew baby boys be killed. A Hebrew mother built a basket, placed her baby boy inside, and sent him out on the Nile River. She prayed someone would find him and keep him safe.

After a while the pharaoh's daughter noticed the basket floating by and peered inside. "Oh my, it's a baby," she said, picking up the child. The baby giggled and smiled. "What a sweet child. I think I will raise this baby as my own."

41

So the child, named Moses, grew up in the palace with the evil pharaoh. As time passed, Moses saw the way the Hebrews were treated by the Egyptians. One day, he witnessed a fight between a guard and a Hebrew. He thought no one was watching, and he pushed the guard, killing him. News spread quickly about what Moses had done, so Moses ran away to live in the desert where he became a shepherd.

Many years later, when Moses was out with his sheep, he saw a bush on fire. The flames were red-hot, but the bush was not burning up. When he got closer, a voice called out, "Moses, I am God! I have seen how the Hebrews suffer. I want you to go to Egypt to save them. I have a beautiful place picked out for them." God gave Moses a beautiful staff that he would use to show the pharaoh God's power.

So Moses went to Egypt just like God told him to. "You need to let the Hebrews go," Moses said to Pharaoh. But Pharaoh just shook his head, no. "Then God will send down a plague every time you say no."

First, the river turned dark red with blood. But Pharaoh said no. Then God sent frogs that hopped into people's houses and got stuck in their food. But still Pharaoh said no. God kept sending plagues until finally Pharaoh said, "Go!"

45

Quickly Moses and the Hebrews gathered up their things and left. But they only made it as far as the Red Sea before Pharaoh changed his mind. He and his army chased after Moses.

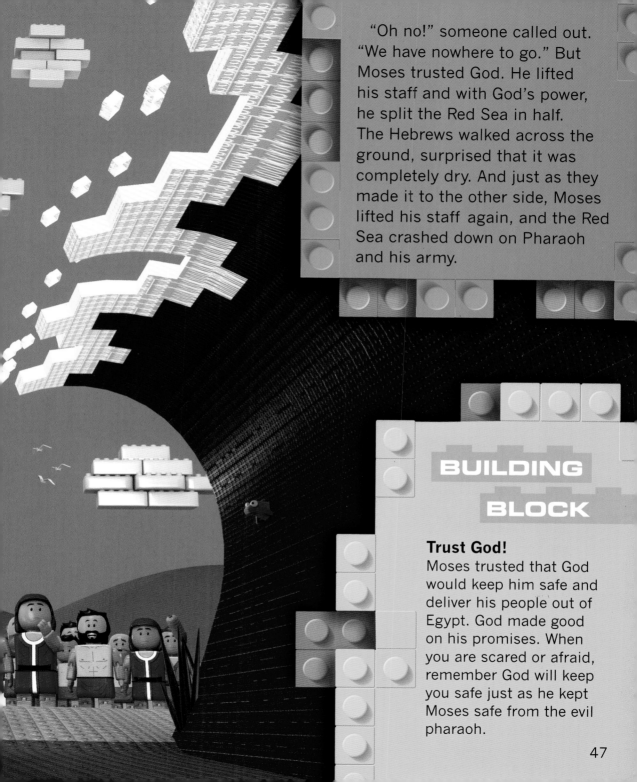

"Oh no!" someone called out. "We have nowhere to go." But Moses trusted God. He lifted his staff and with God's power, he split the Red Sea in half. The Hebrews walked across the ground, surprised that it was completely dry. And just as they made it to the other side, Moses lifted his staff again, and the Red Sea crashed down on Pharaoh and his army.

BUILDING BLOCK

Trust God!

Moses trusted that God would keep him safe and deliver his people out of Egypt. God made good on his promises. When you are scared or afraid, remember God will keep you safe just as he kept Moses safe from the evil pharaoh.

The Wall Breaks

After Moses died, Joshua led the Hebrews. They soon ran into Jericho, a city so strong and so powerful that no one could go through it or around it.

"How are we going to get to the Promised Land?" someone asked.

"I am tired of walking. My feet are sore," another called out.

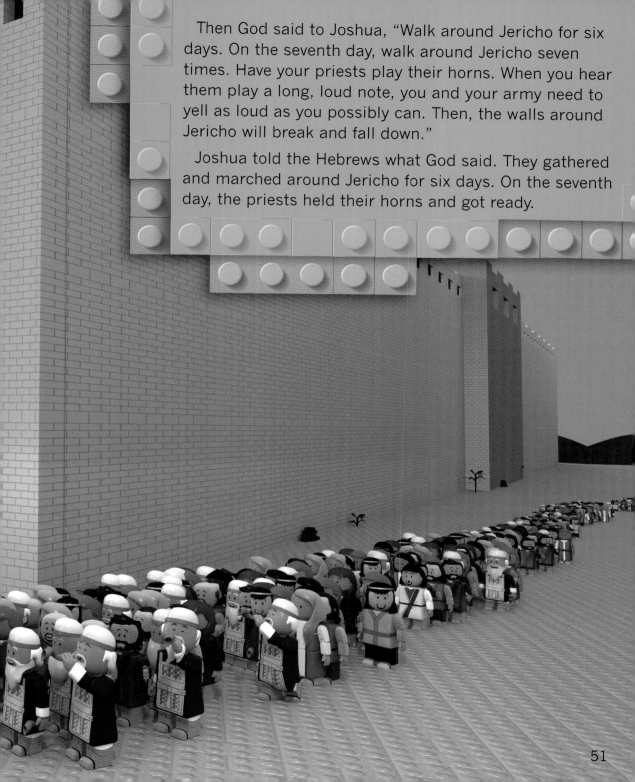

Then God said to Joshua, "Walk around Jericho for six days. On the seventh day, walk around Jericho seven times. Have your priests play their horns. When you hear them play a long, loud note, you and your army need to yell as loud as you possibly can. Then, the walls around Jericho will break and fall down."

Joshua told the Hebrews what God said. They gathered and marched around Jericho for six days. On the seventh day, the priests held their horns and got ready.

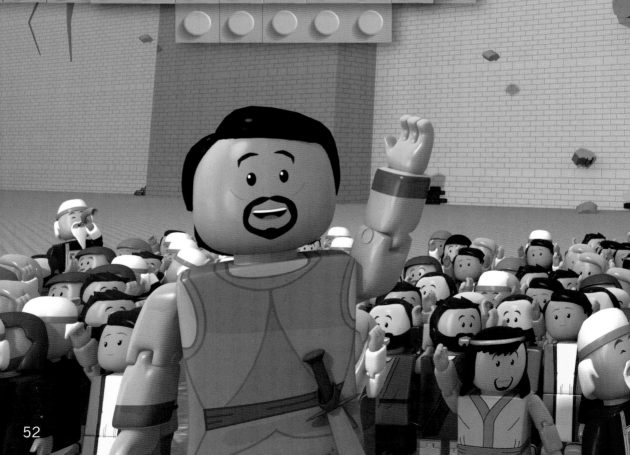

"Do not make a sound until you hear the priests play that long, loud note," Joshua said to the people. "When you do, yell as loud as you possibly can." Then as the Hebrews rounded the walls of Jericho on the seventh day, the first horn played the loudest most beautiful note any of the Hebrews had ever heard. And everyone walking around Jericho opened their mouths and yelled as loud as they possibly could.

The wall around Jericho began to crack. Then, as if God had smashed it with his fists, the wall crumbled to the ground. Joshua and the Hebrews walked straight into Jericho.

BUILDING BLOCK

Obey God!

Joshua did exactly what God told him to do. The walls of Jericho fell down, and Joshua's men charged in and took over the city. Even when there's a difficult obstacle in front of you, listen closely to what God tells you to do. You will overcome it.

Samson's Long Hair

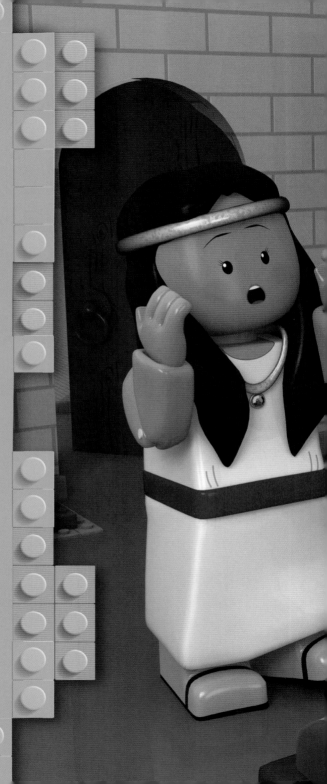

Judges 16

Samson was one of the judges. He was blessed with great strength, but God told him to keep the source of his strength a secret.

Delilah, the woman Samson loved, wanted to know where his strength came from. "Samson, do you love me?" she asked one day. Samson nodded. "Then tell me the secret behind your strength."

Samson said, "You must tie me up with seven bowstrings, then I will become as weak as my enemies." While Samson was asleep, Delilah had him tied up with the bowstrings. When Delilah cried, "Samson! Your enemies are here to kill you!" Samson broke the strings as if they were made of nothing. Delilah was frustrated. She needed to discover the source of Samson's strength. She wanted to earn money promised to her by the Philistines. They planned to kill Samson once his strength was gone.

"You lied to me!" Delilah said, sounding hurt and angry. "You must tell me the truth! Where does your strength come from?" Samson thought about her question and said, "You must tie me up with ropes. Then I will become as weak as my enemies." Delilah called for ropes and tied Samson up. But again, Samson broke free.

Delilah was so angry. She continued to bother Samson until finally he told her the truth: "Delilah, the only way to make me as weak as my enemies is to cut my hair. But you must promise not to tell anyone my secret. My strength is a gift from God." Delilah nodded, but while Samson was asleep, Delilah cut his hair. And all at once, Samson's strength disappeared.

Delilah called for the Philistines, and even though Samson tried to fight back, he had lost all of his strength.

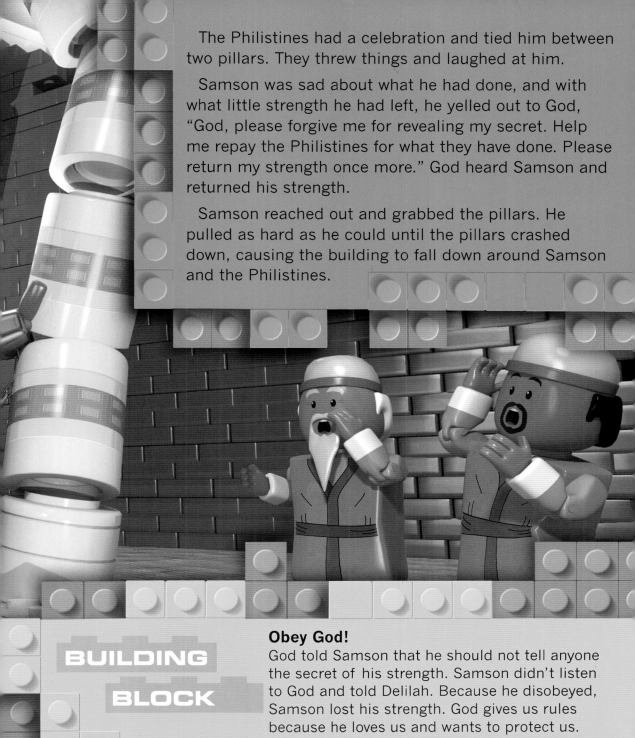

The Philistines had a celebration and tied him between two pillars. They threw things and laughed at him.

Samson was sad about what he had done, and with what little strength he had left, he yelled out to God, "God, please forgive me for revealing my secret. Help me repay the Philistines for what they have done. Please return my strength once more." God heard Samson and returned his strength.

Samson reached out and grabbed the pillars. He pulled as hard as he could until the pillars crashed down, causing the building to fall down around Samson and the Philistines.

BUILDING

BLOCK

Obey God!
God told Samson that he should not tell anyone the secret of his strength. Samson didn't listen to God and told Delilah. Because he disobeyed, Samson lost his strength. God gives us rules because he loves us and wants to protect us. Remember to obey God!

Naomi and Ruth

Ruth 1–4

Naomi's husband and sons died, and she was left with her two daughters-in-law, Orpah and Ruth. It was a time of great famine, but Naomi had heard that there was food in her hometown of Bethlehem. She spoke to Orpah and Ruth, "My children, I am going to Bethlehem. You both should go back to your parents. You do not need to stay with me."

Orpah cried, but agreed that she would return to her parents. Ruth shook her head and said, "No, Naomi. Where you go, I will go. Where you stay, I will stay. Your people will be my people. Your God will be my God." Ruth had made up her mind, and no one, including Naomi, could convince her to stay. So the two women went to Bethlehem.

61

For food, Ruth picked grain in the fields. One day, when Ruth was working hard, the owner of the fields saw her. "Who is that woman?" Boaz asked the man in charge of his workers.

"Her name is Ruth. She came here from Moab with Naomi. She is a strong worker and hardly rests from morning until dusk," the man said. Boaz nodded, smiling at the woman who was such a hard worker.

"Ruth, please, stop picking grain. Walk behind the men and pick up what has fallen on the ground. And when you are tired, rest," Boaz said. Ruth was confused. "Why are you being so nice to me? I am not even from around here," she said.

But Boaz just shook his head and continued, "I heard what you did for Naomi. How you left everything behind to come to Bethlehem with her. May God reward you for all that you have done!"

"Thank you for being kind to me," she said. Ruth was grateful for Boaz's kindness.

64

Eventually, Ruth and Boaz grew close and got married. They had many children, and their great-grandson was King David!

BUILDING BLOCK

Serve God!
God saw how hard Ruth worked to care for and serve Naomi, so he gave her a new family of her own. When you serve others with love and care, you serve God and show him your love.

The Smooth Stone

1 Samuel 17

Goliath was a Philistine warrior. He was nine feet tall and wore shiny bronze armor that flashed in the sunlight. Everyone in the Israelite army was too scared to fight him.

"He's too tall and strong!" one soldier said. "He's too angry!" another cried. But a young boy named David wasn't scared of Goliath. "I will fight the giant," David announced to the soldiers.

Saul, the king of the Israelites, wanted to meet the brave young man. "You called for me?" David said. "Yes, I heard that you think you can fight Goliath," Saul replied. "Yes. I may be small, but I will fight with God by my side," David said confidently. And Saul said, "Go!"

So David went out to a nearby riverbank and collected five stones. He dropped them in the pouch that hung at his side, and he grabbed his slingshot.

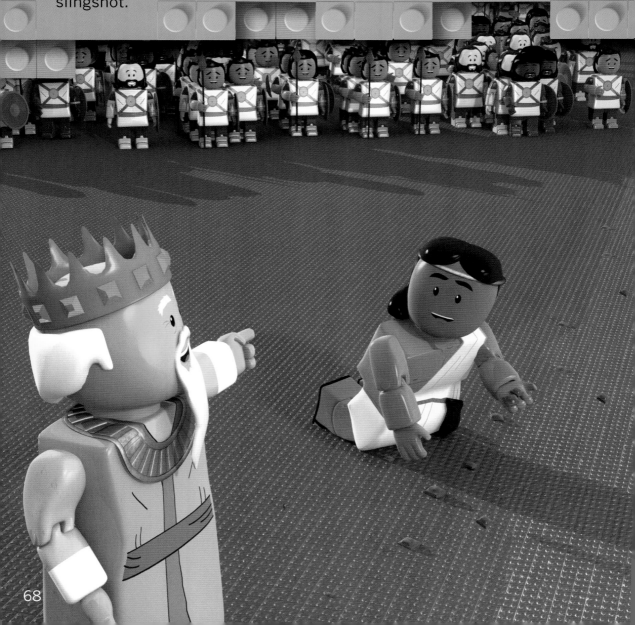

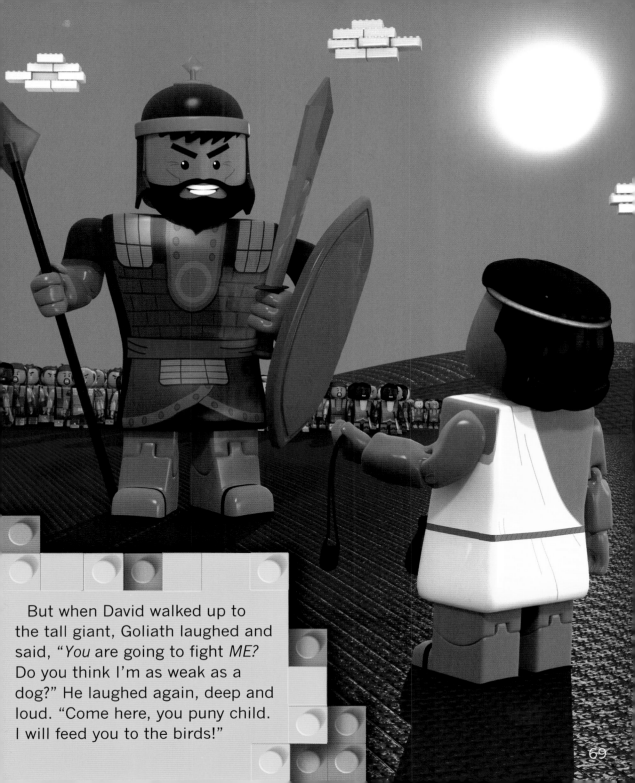

But when David walked up to the tall giant, Goliath laughed and said, "*You* are going to fight *ME?* Do you think I'm as weak as a dog?" He laughed again, deep and loud. "Come here, you puny child. I will feed you to the birds!"

69

David was filled with courage. He said, "You are attacking me with a sword, but I am attacking you in the name of the Lord who rules over everything! I will defeat you, and everyone will know there is only one God in Israel!" David grabbed a single stone from his pouch and placed it in his slingshot. With one quick swing, David threw the stone at Goliath. It hit him directly between his eyes.

Goliath staggered and fell to the ground! David had defeated Goliath with the strength and courage of the one true God of Israel!

Trust God!
David was not afraid, and he defeated Goliath with just a single small stone. Do not be afraid. Just like God protected David, he will help you overcome any struggle.

BUILDING

BLOCK

Building the Temple

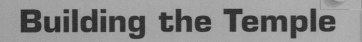

1 Kings 6

Young King Solomon decided to build the most beautiful temple in Jerusalem. He wanted people to go there to worship God.

The temple was built out of strong cedar beams and boulders. The ceilings inside the temple were so high people had to strain their necks to see them. There was even a beautiful porch built in the front of the temple that people could walk out on to enjoy God's great creation.

The builders worked hard building the temple. And when the workers were finally done putting the walls in place, artists went inside and decorated them with amazing works of art.

Solomon had a special room—the Most Holy Place—built inside the temple. The walls were covered with gold, and a beautiful sculpture of two cherubim was placed inside. Their wings spread out as wide as the room, and Solomon had it covered with gold too. Solomon was so happy that he built an altar for the Lord and burned sweet-smelling incense.

Solomon then had the Ark of the Covenant brought into the Most Holy Place. He dedicated the temple to the Lord, making it known across Israel that the temple was for God.

BUILDING BLOCK

Serve God!
Solomon was a wise king, and he loved the Lord. Because Solomon served God with all his heart, more people came to know God. Be like Solomon—wise and ready to serve God.

77

Elijah Builds an Altar

1 Kings 18

Many people worshiped false gods. But Elijah still loved and believed in the one true God of Israel. So Elijah traveled to Ahab's kingdom to share the good news.

"You have turned from the Lord's commandments. You worship a false god called Baal." Ahab heard Elijah, but refused to change his ways. "Fine, I will just have to show you," said Elijah as he gathered some wood to build an altar. He told some of Baal's prophets to gather two bulls.

"Put your bull on the altar, but do not light the fire," Elijah said. "Pray to your gods. Then I will pray to the Lord. The one who lights this altar on fire is the one true God." Ahab agreed to this test.

The prophets put their bull on the altar first, and they screamed as loud as they possibly could, "Baal, hear us! Set this altar on fire!" But nothing happened. So they yelled louder, and they danced around the altar, but still nothing happened.

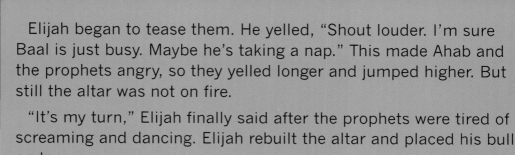

Elijah began to tease them. He yelled, "Shout louder. I'm sure Baal is just busy. Maybe he's taking a nap." This made Ahab and the prophets angry, so they yelled longer and jumped higher. But still the altar was not on fire.

"It's my turn," Elijah finally said after the prophets were tired of screaming and dancing. Elijah rebuilt the altar and placed his bull on top.

Elijah began to pray, "Lord, you are the one true God. Please, let everyone see that you are the God of Israel." Then Elijah called out, "Let them know that I have done all of this because you told me to. Answer me, God, so that these people will know that you are the one true God." And the Lord came down and set the altar on fire.

Everyone who saw it was amazed! They all fell flat on their faces and praised the one true God!

BUILDING BLOCK

Believe in God!
Believe in God, just as Elijah did. He will do amazing things in your life too!

The Fiery Furnace

Daniel 3

King Nebuchadnezzar built a golden, 90-foot statue that everyone in the kingdom was ordered to worship. But three men named Shadrach, Meshach, and Abednego only loved and worshiped the one true God of Israel.

King Nebuchadnezzar was angry with the three men. "Shadrach, Meshach, and Abednego, why won't you bow down before my god?" the king asked. "You must. If you don't, I will throw you into a fiery furnace."

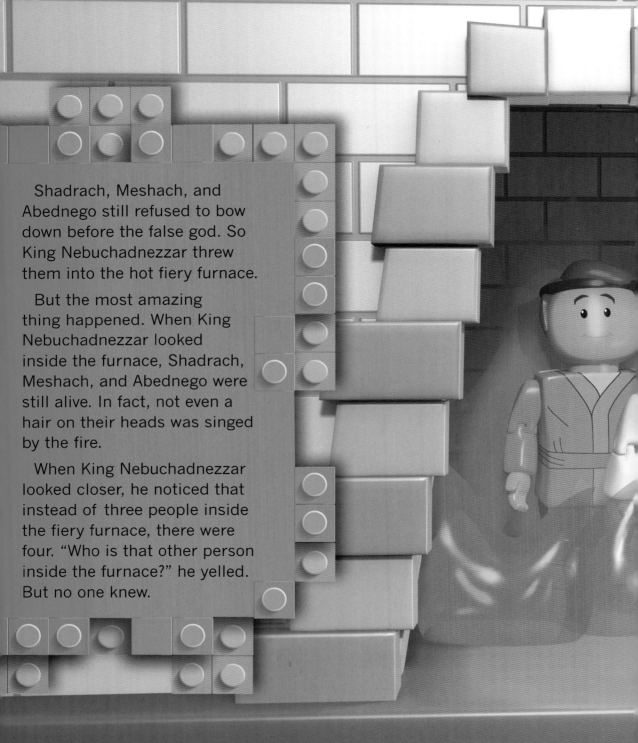

Shadrach, Meshach, and Abednego still refused to bow down before the false god. So King Nebuchadnezzar threw them into the hot fiery furnace.

But the most amazing thing happened. When King Nebuchadnezzar looked inside the furnace, Shadrach, Meshach, and Abednego were still alive. In fact, not even a hair on their heads was singed by the fire.

When King Nebuchadnezzar looked closer, he noticed that instead of three people inside the fiery furnace, there were four. "Who is that other person inside the furnace?" he yelled. But no one knew.

Shocked, King Nebuchadnezzar yelled into the fiery furnace, "Shadrach, Meshach, and Abednego, come out of there." And out walked the three men, unharmed by the fire. "Who was in there with you? I saw four people in the furnace," he said. The men revealed that God had sent an angel to protect them from the flames.

King Nebuchadnezzar knew the one true God was real, and from then on, he followed and worshiped God because of what he had seen.

Obey God!
Shadrach, Meshach, and Abednego obeyed God when they did not bow to King Nebuchadnezzar's giant statue. Because they obeyed, God saved them and showed the king that there is only one God we should worship. God rewards us when we obey him!

BUILDING

BLOCK

Daniel and the Lions

Daniel 6

Daniel loved God and prayed to him three times a day. One day King Darius declared, "Everyone in my kingdom must bow down and pray to me!" But Daniel continued to do what he did every day. He went to his home and prayed to the one true God.

The king's advisors saw Daniel praying to God. So they quickly ran to tell the king what Daniel was doing, "King, King. Listen! Daniel has disobeyed you. He has been praying to God instead of you. You must do something!" King Darius was sad. Daniel was a good friend. But his advisors were right. Daniel had disobeyed him.

"Throw Daniel into the lions' den," King Darius commanded. The advisors went and collected Daniel, who was still praying.

They threw him into the den where lions waited hungrily for their evening meal. King Darius called down to Daniel, "Daniel, you serve your God faithfully. I hope he keeps you safe."

When Daniel landed down in the lions' den, God was with him, and he kept Daniel safe. He closed the lions' mouths and kept their stomachs full. Daniel praised the Lord and prayed, thanking God for keeping him safe.

The next morning, King Darius went to the lions' den to see if God had kept Daniel safe. He was amazed to see Daniel still alive.

94

"Daniel, you do serve the one true God! I will order that everyone must worship the God of Israel!" And so it was that everyone in the kingdom worshiped the one true God.

Trust God!

Daniel did what was right and trusted God. He knew God would keep him safe. Even a pack of hungry lions couldn't harm Daniel because God was on his side. If God can protect Daniel from the lions, he can keep you safe too!

BUILDING BLOCK

95

Jonah and the Big Fish

Jonah 1–3

"Go to Nineveh, Jonah!" God called out. But Jonah did not want to go. The people in Nineveh were scary and behaved badly. So Jonah disobeyed God. He decided to sail to Tarshish instead.

But the Lord saw that Jonah was disobeying him, so he sent a terrible storm. The boat began to rock and roll. The sailors aboard were terrified and didn't know what to do.

"The boat is going to sink!" one sailor yelled.

"The sails are ripping!" another cried out.

But Jonah knew why this was happening. "I have disobeyed God, and this is my punishment. Throw me overboard, or we are all going to die," Jonah said sadly.

97

The sailors agreed it was the only thing to do. They tossed Jonah overboard and the skies immediately cleared. But as soon as Jonah fell into the sea, a big fish appeared and swallowed him whole.

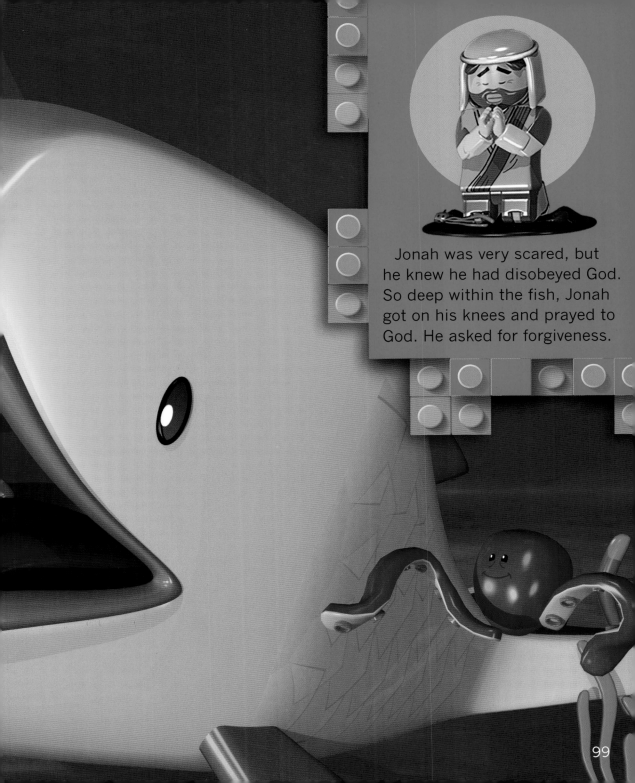

Jonah was very scared, but he knew he had disobeyed God. So deep within the fish, Jonah got on his knees and prayed to God. He asked for forgiveness.

Jonah was in the fish for three days and three nights, and he continued to pray. Then on the third day, God commanded that Jonah be spit out. Jonah went soaring through the air and landed near shore.

Jonah thanked the Lord and headed to Nineveh to share the good news of the one true God.

Obey God!

Jonah was scared to go to Nineveh, so he disobeyed God. But God gave Jonah time to think and pray about his choices. God wants us to serve him with our whole hearts. It makes him happy.

NEW TESTAMENT

Mary and the Bright Angel

Luke 1:26–38

Mary was a young girl who lived in the town of Nazareth. Mary loved God more than anything.

One day, Mary was visited by an angel as bright as the sun. The angel's name was Gabriel.

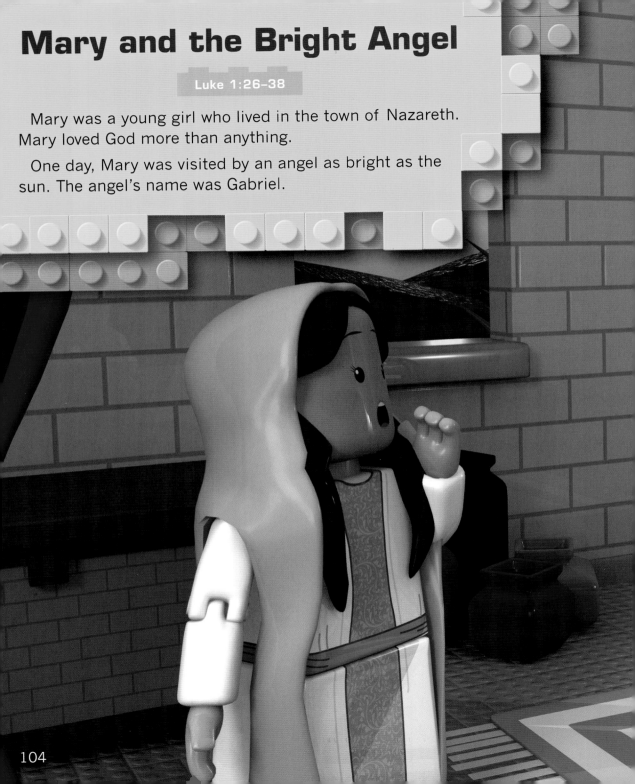

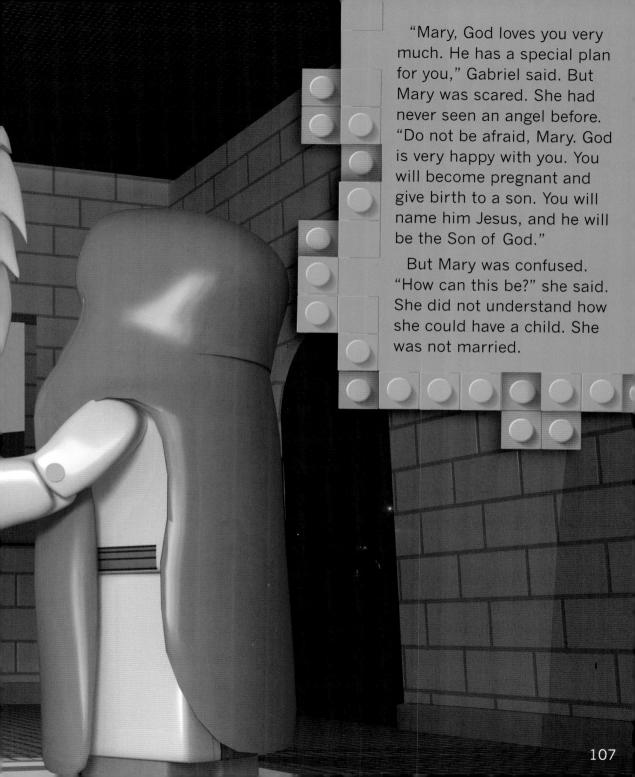

"Mary, God loves you very much. He has a special plan for you," Gabriel said. But Mary was scared. She had never seen an angel before. "Do not be afraid, Mary. God is very happy with you. You will become pregnant and give birth to a son. You will name him Jesus, and he will be the Son of God."

But Mary was confused. "How can this be?" she said. She did not understand how she could have a child. She was not married.

"Do not worry, Mary. God is wonderful, mighty, and powerful," Gabriel said. "Nothing is impossible for God." Gabriel smiled at Mary, and the bright light that shone from him made Mary smile too.

Mary understood what Gabriel said. She trusted God with all her heart. "I love and serve the Lord," she said.

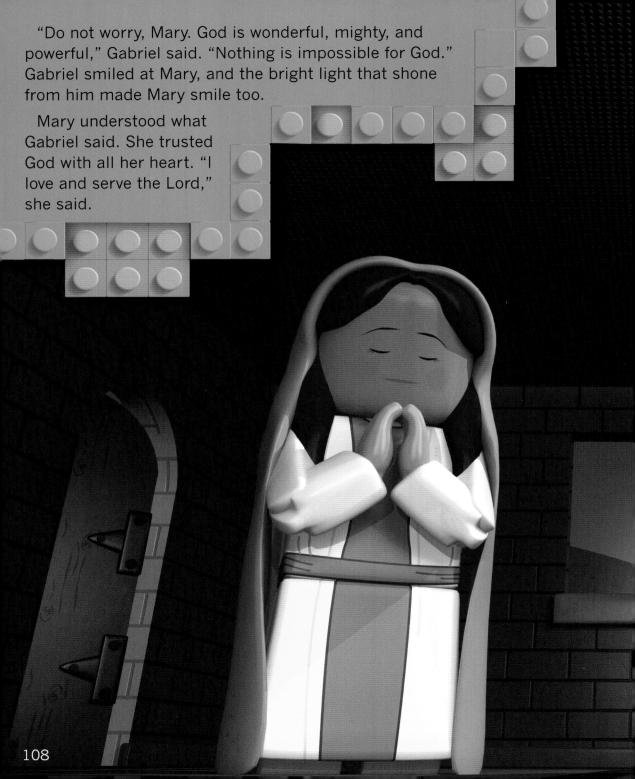

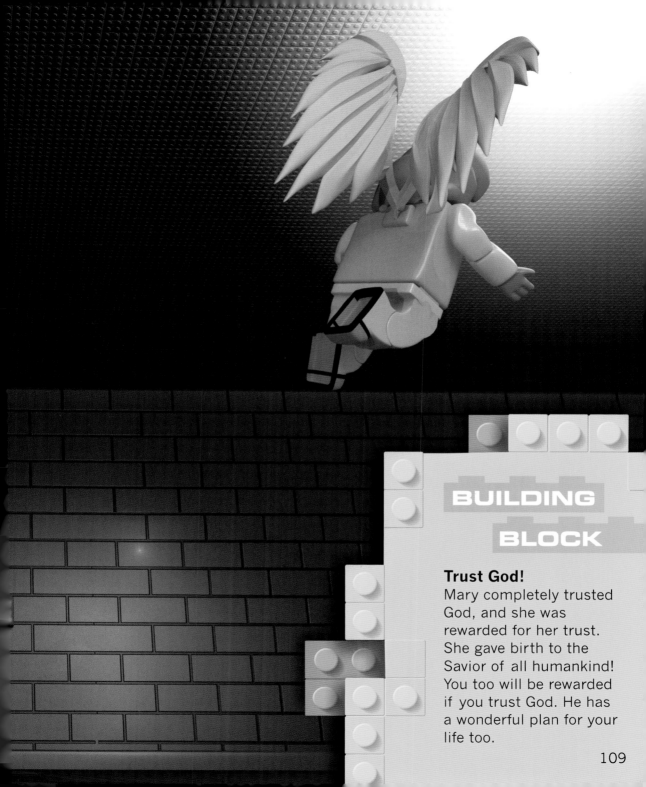

BUILDING BLOCK

Trust God!
Mary completely trusted
God, and she was
rewarded for her trust.
She gave birth to the
Savior of all humankind!
You too will be rewarded
if you trust God. He has
a wonderful plan for your
life too.

109

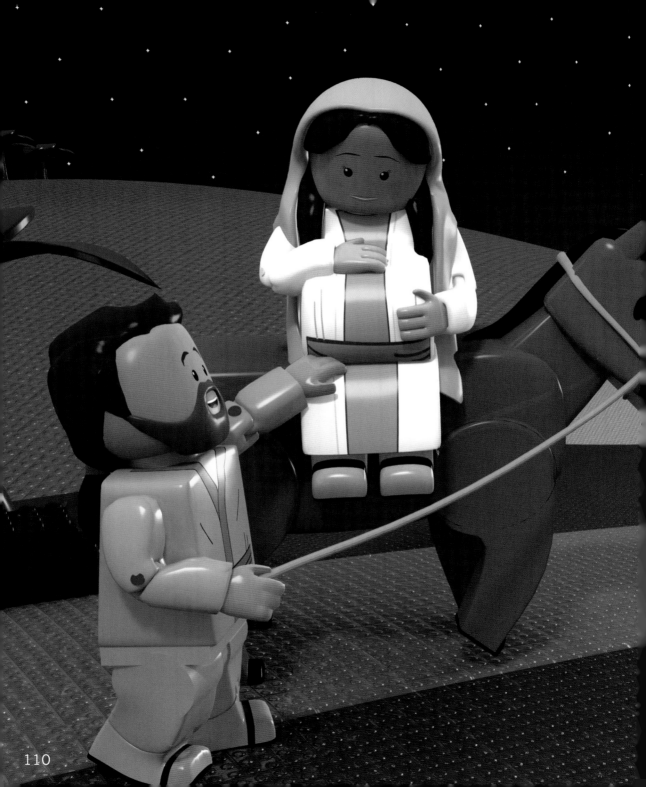

Jesus Is Born!

Luke 2:1–7

Mary was married to a kind man named Joseph. As the time for her baby's birth drew near, Mary and Joseph had to travel to Bethlehem to be counted.

Mary rode on a small brown donkey all the way to Bethlehem. But when they arrived, there was no place for them to sleep.

111

"I am sorry, but this inn is full," one innkeeper said.

"There is no place for you to sleep here," said another.

Finally, an innkeeper offered them a place to stay, "I have no room at the inn, but you can sleep in the stable where my sheep and cows sleep." So Mary and Joseph went into the stable where cows and horses slept in the hay.

Mary looked around the stable and smiled. It was a perfect place to have her baby. It was warm amongst the animals, and the manger would make a nice soft bed for her baby to sleep.

BUILDING BLOCK

Believe in Jesus!
God had been planning the birth of Jesus for a long time. When Jesus was born in a tiny stable, God's plans for him were anything but small. Believe that he is your savior and stay strong in that belief.

115

The Shepherds See a Bright Angel

Luke 2:8–20

In a field nearby, there were shepherds watching over their sheep. Suddenly, a bright angel appeared in the night sky and declared wonderful news. "Do not be afraid. I bring great news," said the angel. "In Bethlehem, a Savior has been born! He is the Messiah! You will know it is him. He will be wrapped in cloth and lying in a manger."

Then, all at once, a group of bright angels appeared over the shepherds. They praised God, singing, "Glory to God in the highest. Peace to all mankind!"

The shepherds were so excited. They shouted and ran to Bethlehem to see the baby. When they found Mary and Joseph in the stable, they were filled with joy. A sweet, small baby was lying in a manger. He looked up at the shepherds and smiled.

The shepherds left to share the good news of the newborn King.

Praise the Lord!
Every day, not just at Christmas, join the angels and shepherds in song, and worship God, for he has given us Jesus who will save us from our sins.

BUILDING

BLOCK

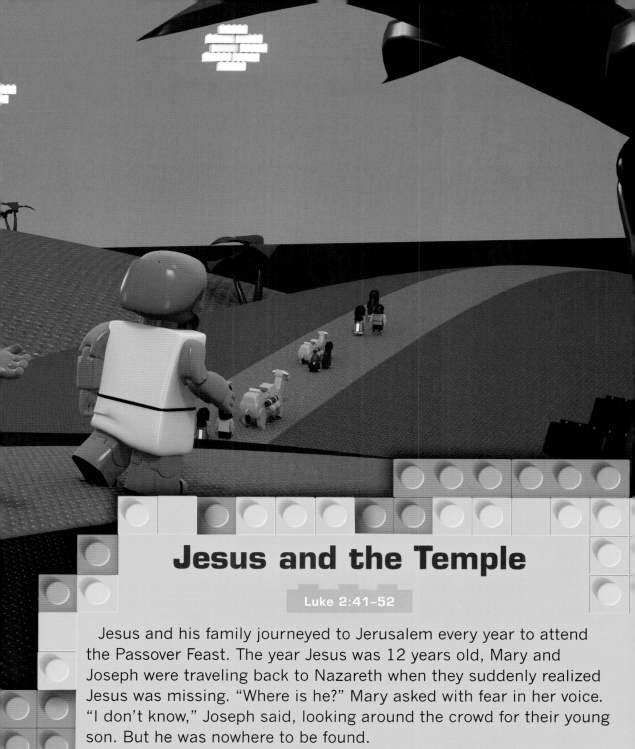

Jesus and the Temple

Luke 2:41–52

Jesus and his family journeyed to Jerusalem every year to attend the Passover Feast. The year Jesus was 12 years old, Mary and Joseph were traveling back to Nazareth when they suddenly realized Jesus was missing. "Where is he?" Mary asked with fear in her voice. "I don't know," Joseph said, looking around the crowd for their young son. But he was nowhere to be found.

123

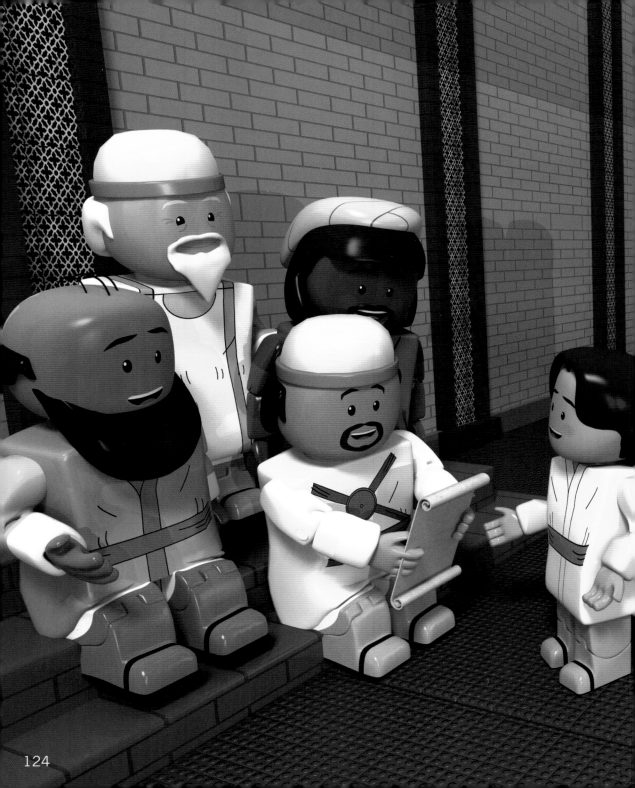

In a panic, Mary and Joseph went back to Jerusalem to search for him. Finally, they found Jesus in the temple. Jesus was safe and listening to the teachers, asking them interesting questions. And the people who heard him were surprised by how intelligent and wise he was.

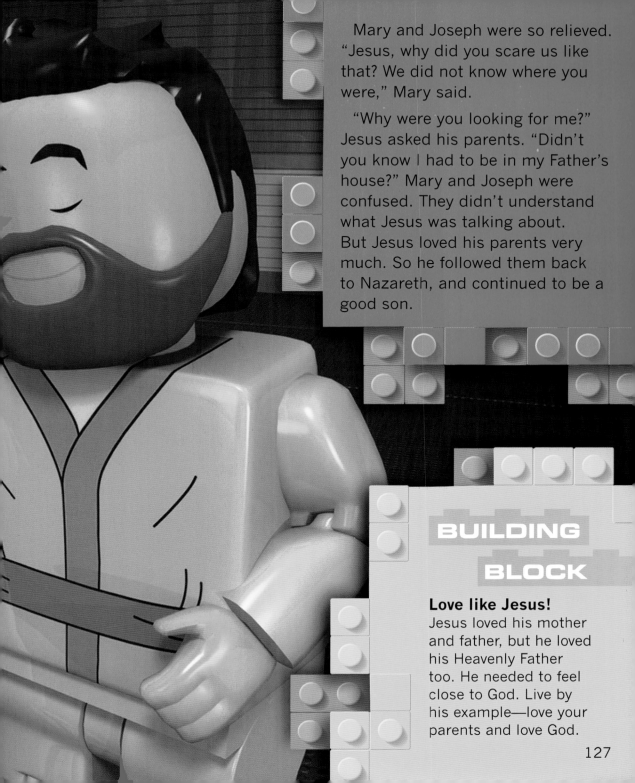

Mary and Joseph were so relieved. "Jesus, why did you scare us like that? We did not know where you were," Mary said.

"Why were you looking for me?" Jesus asked his parents. "Didn't you know I had to be in my Father's house?" Mary and Joseph were confused. They didn't understand what Jesus was talking about. But Jesus loved his parents very much. So he followed them back to Nazareth, and continued to be a good son.

BUILDING

BLOCK

Love like Jesus!
Jesus loved his mother and father, but he loved his Heavenly Father too. He needed to feel close to God. Live by his example—love your parents and love God.

127

John the Baptist and Jesus

Matthew 3:1–17

John the Baptist was Jesus' cousin. He told people about the good news of Jesus. "Try not to sin, the Messiah is coming," he preached.

"I'm sorry for the mean things I have done," people often said to John. And John would baptize them in the Jordan River.

"I baptize you in water. But remember that someone is coming who will forgive you of all of your sins," John would say.

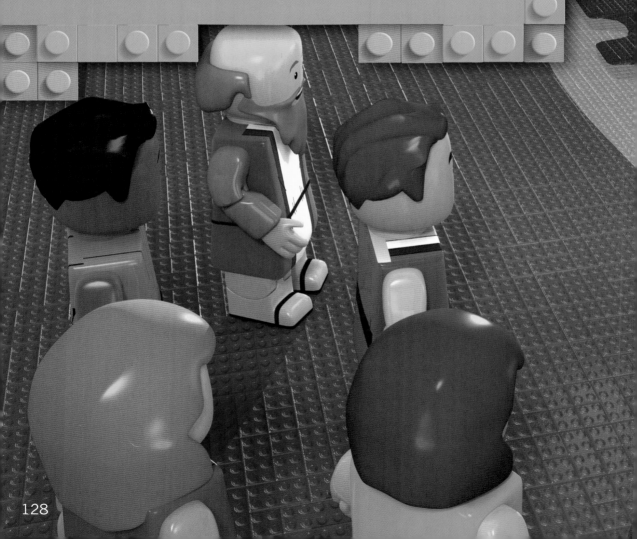

Then one day Jesus came to the river where John was preaching. "John, I need you to baptize me," Jesus said. But John was surprised. He didn't understand. "That cannot be, Jesus," John said. "You should baptize me."

But Jesus told John that it was God's plan. John must baptize Jesus.

So Jesus was baptized in the beautiful waters of the Jordan River. As he came up out of the water, a white dove flew down from the sky. "This is my Son, and I love him," said a voice from heaven.

Spread the Good News!

Just like John the Baptist, go out and tell your friends, and the world if you are able, that Jesus has saved us all from our sins. If we believe in him, we will live in heaven forever with Jesus.

BUILDING BLOCK

133

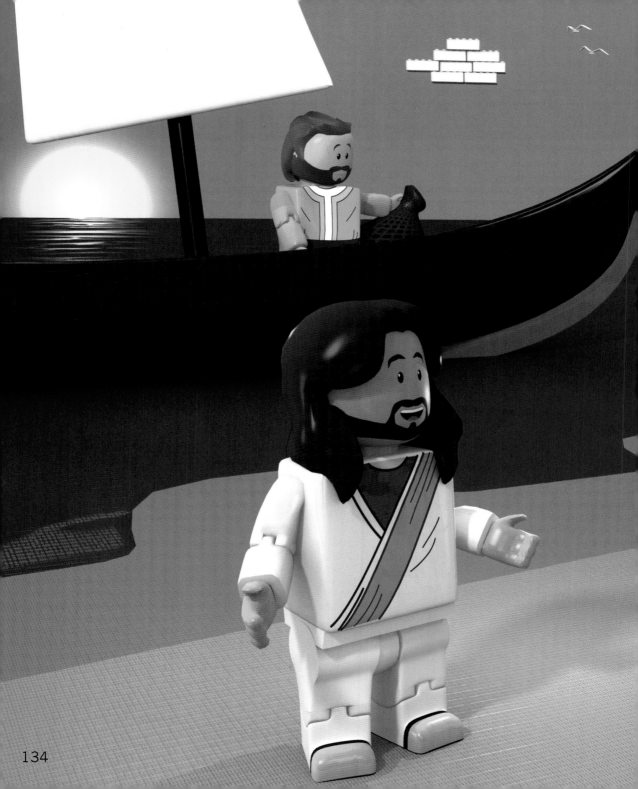

Fishing for People

Luke 5:1–11

Jesus was standing on the golden, sandy beach of the Sea of Galilee. He was talking to a large crowd of people who had come to listen to him.

Jesus spotted two fishing boats near the shore. "Simon, go out into the deep water and drop your fishing nets," Jesus said to the fisherman. But Simon was tired. He had been fishing all day long. "Sir, I haven't caught anything, but I guess since you asked, I will give it one last try," Simon said.

So Simon dropped the nets into the deep blue water and waited. All at once, tons of purple and pink and orange fish began jumping into Simon's nets. There were so many fish that the nets almost split in half. So Simon called to the other boat, "Come, help us catch all of these fish!"

The other boat sailed over, and the two boats pulled in so many fish that their boats began to sink. Simon was amazed by what he was seeing.

When they returned to shore Simon knelt before Jesus.

"I am a sinner. I do not deserve to be with you," he said. But Jesus loved Simon. And Jesus said, "Do not be afraid. From now on you will fish for people."

And Simon, James, and John left everything behind and followed Jesus.

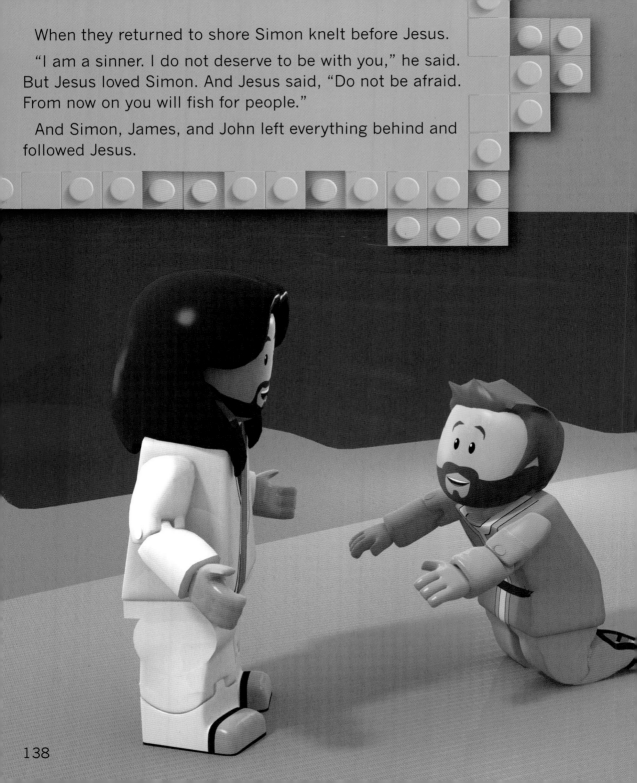

Spread the Good News!

Jesus found twelve disciples to help him teach and share the good news of salvation. Go out and share the good news of eternal life with the people you know like Jesus and his disciples did.

BUILDING

BLOCK

Jesus and the Storm

Mark 4:35–41

Jesus and his disciples were in need of rest. So Jesus said, "Let's go over to the other side of the lake."

As Jesus and his friends set sail, strong winds began to blow and the sky grew dark. Rough waves crashed against their boat, and the men were afraid. But Jesus had fallen asleep, and he didn't hear the storm.

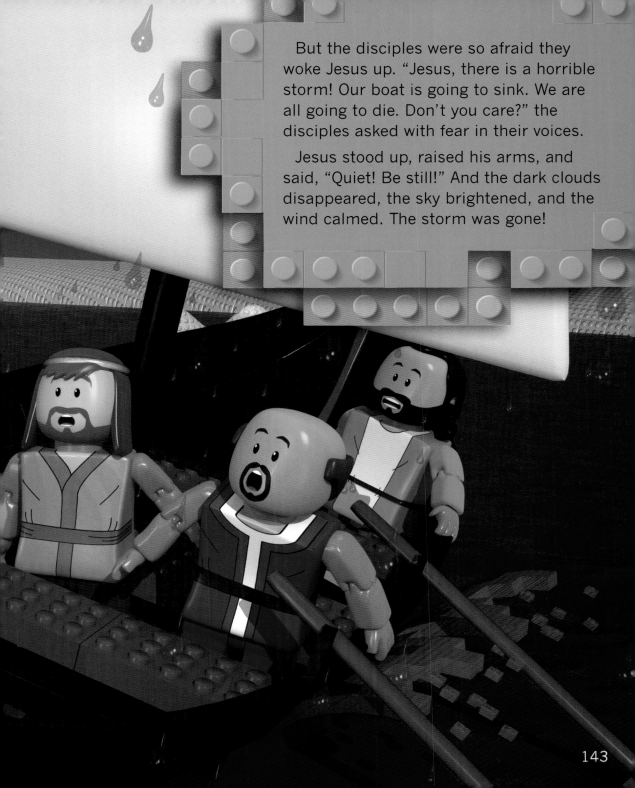

But the disciples were so afraid they woke Jesus up. "Jesus, there is a horrible storm! Our boat is going to sink. We are all going to die. Don't you care?" the disciples asked with fear in their voices.

Jesus stood up, raised his arms, and said, "Quiet! Be still!" And the dark clouds disappeared, the sky brightened, and the wind calmed. The storm was gone!

143

"Why were you so afraid? Don't you have any faith at all?" Jesus asked the men. They looked at each other, still shocked by what they had seen.

"Who is this man?" one disciple asked.

"Even the winds and the sea obey him," another disciple said.

They could not believe what they had witnessed.

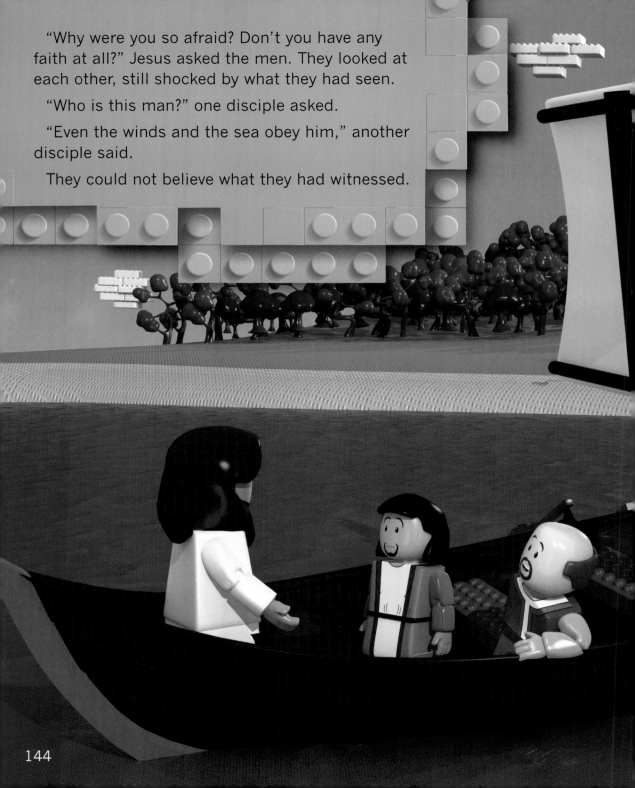

BUILDING
BLOCK

Trust Jesus!
Jesus stopped a storm
with a single word. He
told the disciples to trust
that he would take care
of them no matter what.
You can trust Jesus in the
same way.

Jesus, the Loaves, and the Fish

Matthew 14:13–21

Jesus was speaking to a large crowd all day. The people loved to hear him speak, but they were growing hungry.

"Jesus, there is nothing here for these people to eat," one disciple said.

"It is getting late. Should we send them home to have dinner?" another disciple asked.

But Jesus wasn't finished speaking. "They don't need to go home. Just give them something to eat," he said.

"But we only have five loaves of bread and two fish," the disciples answered, holding up the golden loaves of bread and the juicy pieces of fish that a young boy offered to share.

Jesus knew what to do with the food. He smiled and took the loaves and fish. He broke the bread and fish into smaller pieces and gave them to the disciples. As they passed the food around they were surprised to see that there was more than enough food to feed all the people. There were even 12 baskets of leftover food after everyone had finished eating.

Believe in Jesus!
Jesus was able to feed 5,000 people with only two fish and five loaves of bread. If Jesus can feed 5,000 people, then we can be sure he will care for all our problems, for he can do amazing things!

BUILDING
BLOCK

149

Jesus Walks on Water

Matthew 14:22–33

Jesus' disciples were out in a boat on the Sea of Galilee when the wind became wild. Tall waves hit the side of the boat, rocking it from side to side.

Suddenly, one of the disciples noticed something in the waves.

"Look," the disciple yelled, pointing to a tall figure that was coming towards them.

"Is that a ghost?" one disciple said, thinking his eyes must be deceiving him. He saw through the mist of seawater that a man was walking on top of the water. The other disciples noticed the man too, and they became afraid. They yelled out in fear.

151

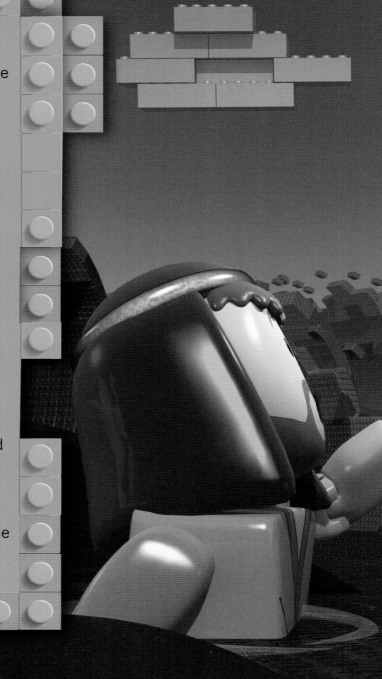

But the man called out to them, "Do not be afraid," he said. As the disciples heard the man's voice, one thought he recognized it.

"Jesus, is that you?" Peter asked. "If it is you, tell me to walk out on the water toward you."

And Jesus said, "Come."

Peter carefully stepped out of the boat and miraculously began to walk on top of the water toward Jesus. But as Peter felt the wind and saw a huge wave beside him, he became afraid. Peter took his eyes off Jesus and began to sink into the water.

"Jesus, save me!" Peter cried out as he sank.

Jesus reached down and grabbed Peter's hand. "Your faith is small," Jesus said as he held on to Peter. "Why did you doubt me?"

Jesus helped Peter back into the boat and climbed in after him. And suddenly, just as it had started, the wind stopped and the waves fell. The disciples worshiped Jesus. "You are the Son of God," they said.

Trust Jesus!
With Jesus to guide him, Peter was able to do something that seemed impossible. He walked on water! Trust in Jesus and keep your eyes on him and you can do things that may seem impossible.

BUILDING

BLOCK

155

The Good Samaritan

Luke 10:25–37

One day, Jesus was talking to a large crowd. A man in the crowd tried to trick Jesus with a hard question.

"Jesus," the man said. "What do I have to do to get into heaven?"

"Love the Lord with all your heart, with all your soul, all your mind, and all your strength," Jesus said. "And love your neighbor as you love yourself."

But the man wasn't satisfied with Jesus' answer. "Who is my neighbor?" the man asked.

"Let me tell you a story," Jesus said.

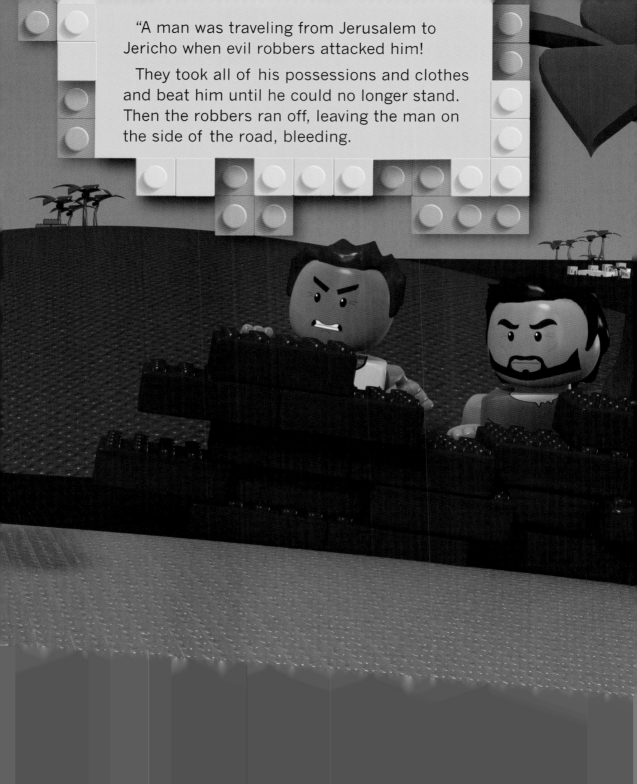

"A man was traveling from Jerusalem to Jericho when evil robbers attacked him!

They took all of his possessions and clothes and beat him until he could no longer stand. Then the robbers ran off, leaving the man on the side of the road, bleeding.

As the man lay there hurt, a priest was traveling down the road. He saw the poor man, but instead of helping him, the priest crossed the road and kept on walking.

Then a Levite came upon the bleeding man. But he did the same thing as the priest. He kept on walking.

Finally, a Samaritan was walking down the road. When he saw the man, he felt sorry for him. The Samaritan knelt down and tended to his wounds. He poured oil and wine on the man's scrapes, and he wrapped bandages around the cuts to stop the bleeding.

Then, with kindness in his heart, the Samaritan picked up the man and placed him on his donkey. He took the man to an inn.

The next day, the Samaritan took two silver coins from his pocket and gave them to the innkeeper.

"Take care of this man," he said.

Jesus finished telling the story and turned back to the man who asked the question.

"Which of the three travelers do you think was a neighbor to the man who was attacked by the robbers?" Jesus asked.

"The Samaritan," the man said.

"Go and be like the Samaritan," Jesus said.

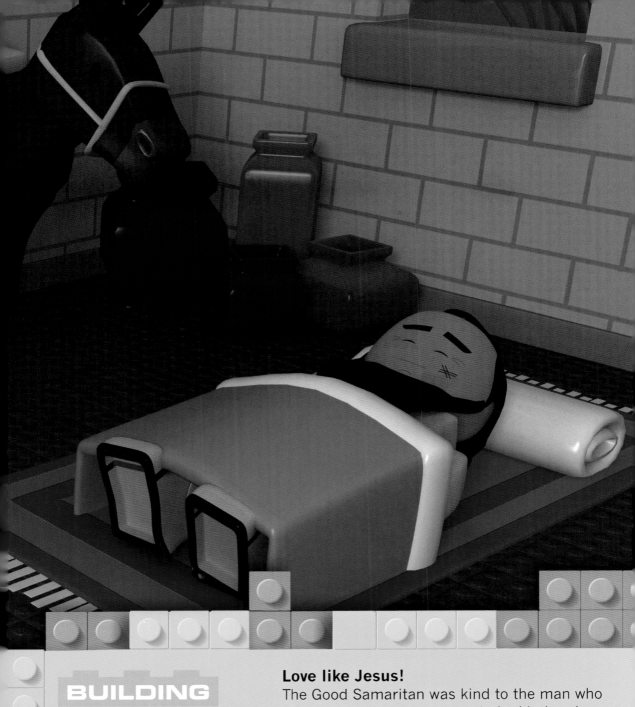

BUILDING
BLOCK

Love like Jesus!
The Good Samaritan was kind to the man who was in pain. Jesus wants us to be kind and loving too. He wants us to live by his example.

Jesus and Lazarus

John 11:1–44

One of Jesus' good friends was named Lazarus. He had two sisters whose names were Mary and Martha. They were Jesus' friends too.

One day, Jesus received a message from Mary and Martha. Lazarus was very sick. He was going to die if Jesus didn't come to heal him.

Jesus loved Lazarus very much and didn't want him to die. But Jesus stayed where he was for three more days. "Do not worry," he said to his disciples, who wondered why he did not go to Lazarus right away.

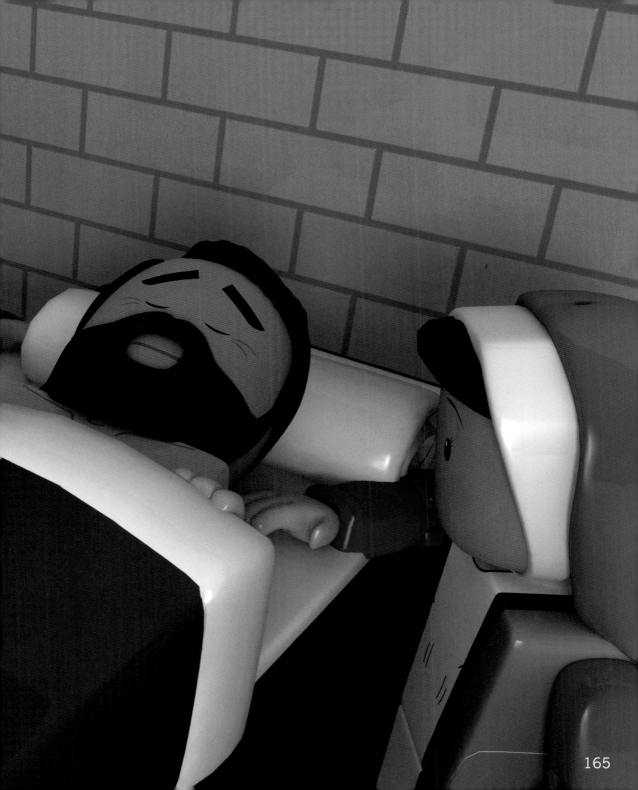

Finally, Jesus went to Mary and Martha, and when he arrived, Martha ran out to meet him.

"Oh, Jesus, you are too late. Lazarus is dead! If you had come sooner, you could have healed my brother," Martha cried.

But Jesus said to her, "Martha, your brother will live again."

Martha went and got her sister Mary. When Jesus saw how sad Mary was, he cried with her. But Jesus was about to do something very special.

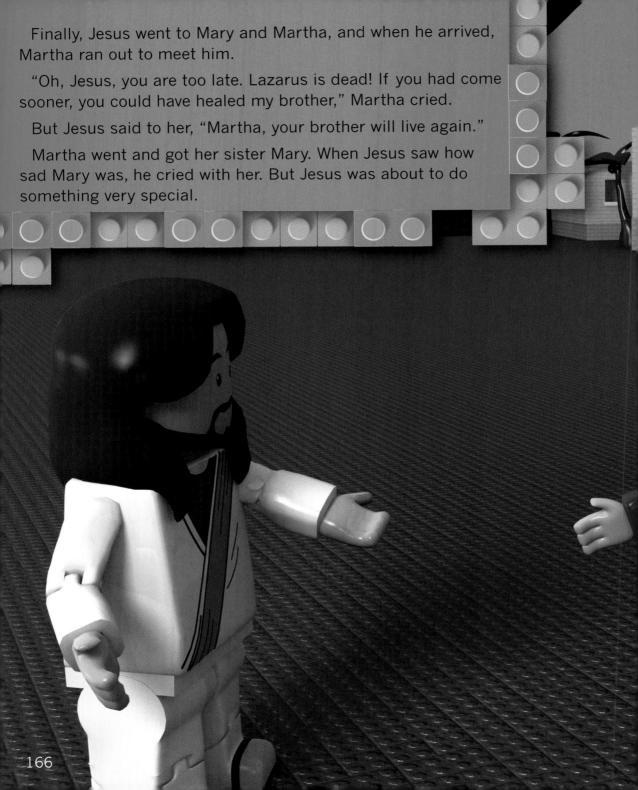

He went to the tomb where Lazarus' body was placed. He had them roll away the stone from in front of the entrance.

"Jesus, my brother's body has been in the tomb for days. It will smell," Martha said.

But Jesus had a magnificent plan, one that would surprise everyone. And Jesus looked up into heaven and said, "God, thank you for listening. I know that you are always with me. I say this now so that those around me will believe that you are almighty." Then Jesus yelled, "Lazarus, come out!"

And out walked Lazarus! He was wrapped in white strips of cloth from head to toe. His sisters ran to help him. Everyone who saw was amazed. They all believed in Jesus!

BUILDING BLOCK

Believe in Jesus!
Everyone thought Lazarus was dead. But Jesus knew that God could do all things, even bring Lazarus back to life. Believe in Jesus and amazing things can happen!

169

Jesus and the Lepers

Luke 17:11-19

Jesus was traveling and teaching about the wonderful news of everlasting life when he came across ten lepers. The lepers were covered with red and pink sores that burned and ached. The men were always in pain and had to cover their skin with strips of cloth.

When they saw Jesus, they yelled out to him, "Jesus, please heal us. We've heard about what you can do. Please do the same for us."

Jesus saw how much pain the lepers were in and said, "Go. Show yourselves to the priests."

The lepers left in a hurry, and as they ran to see the priests, they realized their skin was healed. The red and pink sores were gone. They were amazed and so happy to finally be free of pain!

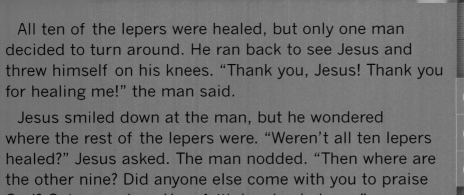

All ten of the lepers were healed, but only one man
decided to turn around. He ran back to see Jesus and
threw himself on his knees. "Thank you, Jesus! Thank you
for healing me!" the man said.

Jesus smiled down at the man, but he wondered
where the rest of the lepers were. "Weren't all ten lepers
healed?" Jesus asked. The man nodded. "Then where are
the other nine? Did anyone else come with you to praise
God? Get up and go. Your faith has healed you."

BUILDING

BLOCK

Pray to God!
Jesus was very happy with the one man who came back to thank him. Pray to God and thank him for all of your blessings too. It will make him very happy.

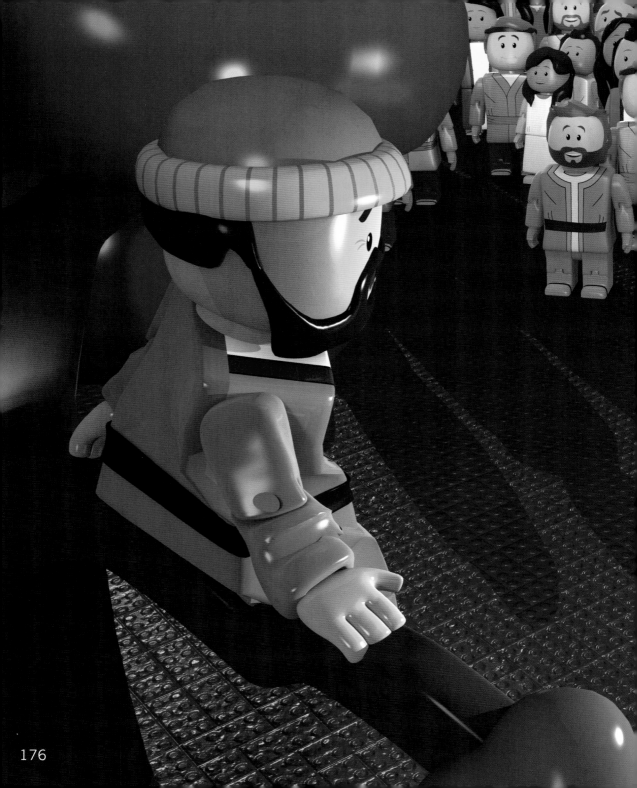

Jesus and Zacchaeus

Luke 19:1–10

One day while Jesus was walking through Jericho, he looked up into a tree. Up in the branches sat a man named Zacchaeus. He was too short to see over the crowds of people who had come to see Jesus. So he had climbed up the tree to get a better view.

"Zacchaeus," Jesus called up to the short man. Zacchaeus looked around, not quite believing that Jesus was talking to him. "Zacchaeus, come down out of that tree. I want to spend some time at your house."

177

Zaccheus scrambled out of the tree and stood in front of Jesus. A wide, bright smile spread across his face.

Now, Zaccheus wasn't just an ordinary man with an ordinary job. He was a tax collector. That meant he took money from people and gave it to the ruler. He often took more money than he was supposed to, and he kept the extra for himself. People didn't like Zaccheus, and they were surprised when Jesus wanted to stay at a tax collector's house.

Zacchaeus was surprised too. He knew that what he did was wrong, and when Jesus got to his house, Zacchaeus said, "I'm sorry. I will give money to the poor. And I will pay back anyone I have cheated. I will even give them more money than I took." Zacchaeus knew that Jesus was an important person, and he wanted to be like Jesus.

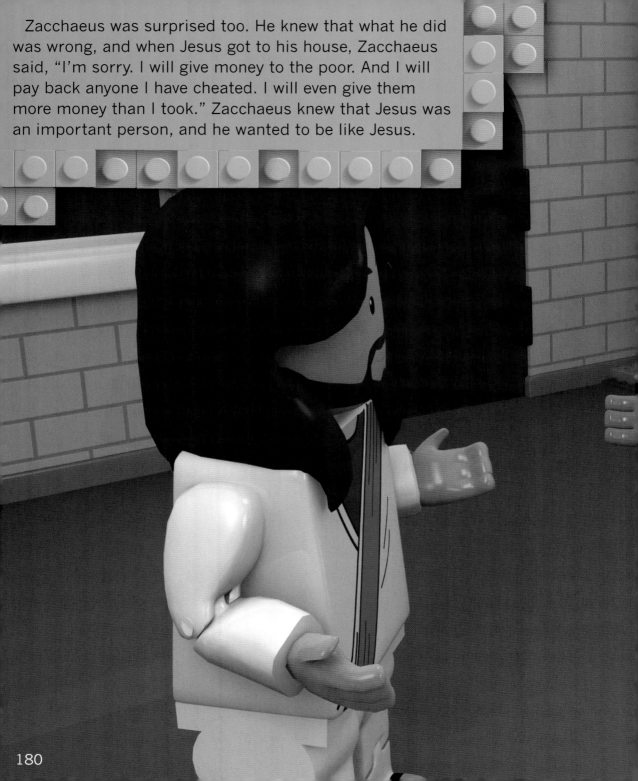

BUILDING
BLOCK

Love like Jesus!
Jesus loved Zacchaeus even though he did bad things. Because Jesus loved him, Zacchaeus decided to change his life and do good for others. You too can show God's love by loving the way Jesus loved Zacchaeus.

181

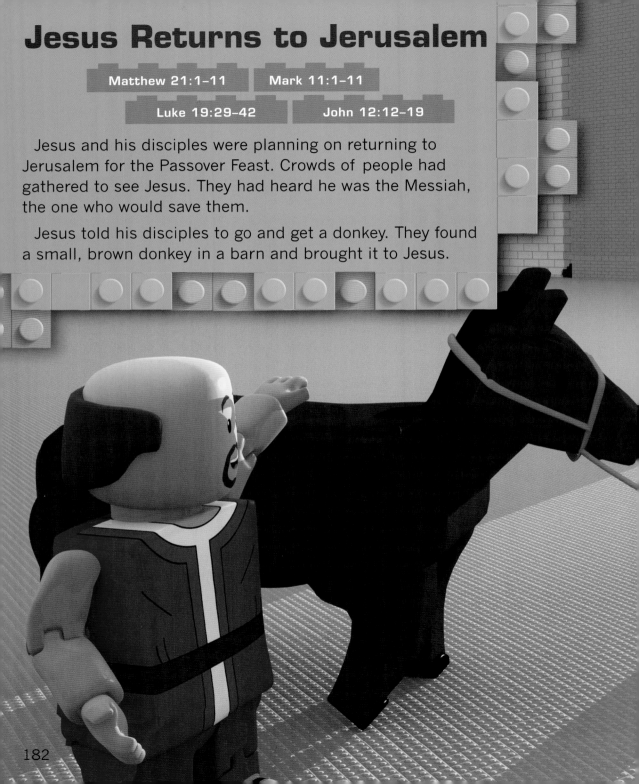

Jesus Returns to Jerusalem

Matthew 21:1–11   Mark 11:1–11

Luke 19:29–42   John 12:12–19

Jesus and his disciples were planning on returning to Jerusalem for the Passover Feast. Crowds of people had gathered to see Jesus. They had heard he was the Messiah, the one who would save them.

Jesus told his disciples to go and get a donkey. They found a small, brown donkey in a barn and brought it to Jesus.

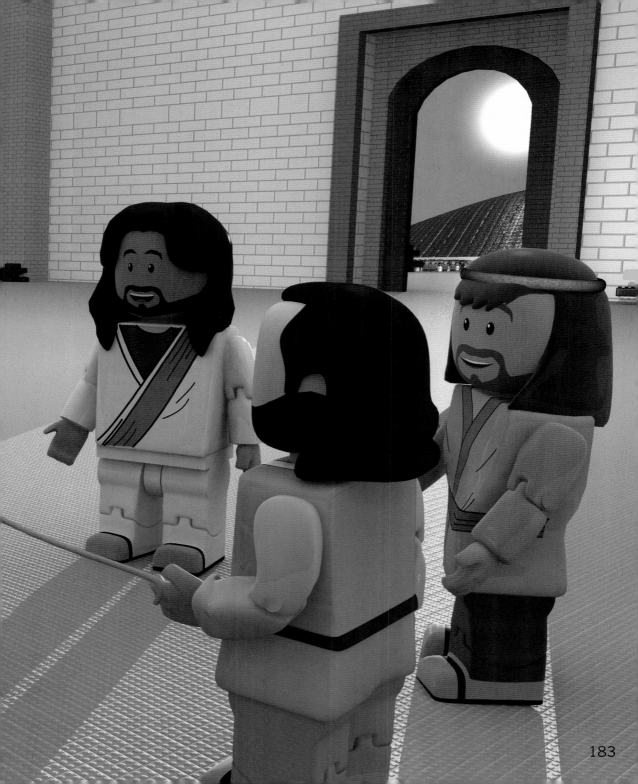

As Jesus rode into Jerusalem his disciples could barely see him through the crowds. Joy filled the air! The people were smiling and yelling, "Hosanna, blessed is the king of Israel!" And in their hands they held long green palm branches that they waved up and down to welcome Jesus into the city.

It was quite a sight to see. But the Pharisees were not happy with Jesus. They were jealous that he was getting so much attention. They agreed that they would have to do something before all the people declared Jesus their king.

BUILDING BLOCK

Praise Jesus!
When we give thanks and praise to Jesus, we can experience joy just like the people of Jerusalem. What are some things you are grateful for today? We have many things we can give praise and sing "Hosanna" to God for in our lives.

Jesus and the Last Supper

Luke 22:7–23

It came time for Jesus to teach his disciples an important lesson. It was time for the Passover Feast, and Jesus sat down at the table to eat with his friends.

"I have been looking forward to eating with all of you," Jesus said to his disciples. "This will be the last meal we will share together."

The disciples looked at one another, worried. They did not understand.

Jesus took a loaf of warm golden bread and broke it in half. He said, "Take this bread and eat it. It is my body broken for you. And every time you eat it, remember me." He handed each disciple a piece of golden brown bread, and they ate it.

Then Jesus took a cup of sweet red wine and shared it. He said, "This cup is a new promise. It is my blood poured out for you. But one of you is going to betray me. And he is here at this table."

The disciples couldn't believe what Jesus was saying. They tried to figure out who would want to betray him. But someone already had.

BUILDING BLOCK

Believe in Jesus!
Jesus promised to lay down his life for the disciples so they would not have to be punished for their sins. Jesus' friends would always remember what Jesus had done for them. It's important for us to remember and believe.

Jesus in the Green Garden

Matthew 26:36-50

Jesus and his disciples went to a garden called Gethsemane. Jesus left his disciples and walked to a spot where he could look out across the garden to see God's beautiful creation. But Jesus was sad. He needed to pray to his Father for help.

"Father, do I really have to die? Can you take this cup of suffering away from me?" But Jesus knew in his heart that God was going to do something wonderful, something important with his death. "If it is not possible, then let your will be done."

Jesus returned to his disciples. They were asleep. Jesus continued to pray for strength and courage. And then he heard footsteps. Jesus called to his disciples, "The time has come. I will be handed over to sinners. Get up. Here comes the one who is going to betray me."

The disciples looked up to see Judas walking through the garden with soldiers and the chief priests. They were coming to arrest Jesus.

Judas walked forward and kissed Jesus on the cheek.

"Friend, do what you came here to do," Jesus said. And the guards arrested Jesus.

BUILDING

BLOCK

Pray to God!
Jesus prayed to God to take away his fear. God answered his prayer and sent an angel to give Jesus strength to face what was about to come. Pray to God whenever you are scared. He will give you strength and courage, just like he gave Jesus the strength to face something very difficult.

193

Jesus Dies on the Cross

Matthew 27:32-56

Luke 23:26-49

Jesus was forced to carry his cross up a steep hill. Guards whipped him and yelled at him. Jesus fell under the weight of the heavy wood.

When Jesus reached the top of the hill, the guards nailed Jesus' hands and feet to the cross. They raised the cross, and as Jesus looked out, he saw there were two criminals, one on either side of him. They were also nailed to crosses.

"Father, forgive them. They do not know what they're doing," Jesus whispered as the soldiers stood near the cross.

Many people were at the crucifixion. Jesus heard people say, "You say you are the Son of God. Then save yourself!" and "Come down from the cross."

Even the chief priests yelled at Jesus. "He saved others, but he can't save himself!"

The skies darkened and clouds hovered over the hill. Jesus looked up into the sky and cried out, "Father, I give you my spirit!" Then Jesus took a deep breath, and he died.

At the same time, in the temple in Jerusalem, the curtain was torn right down the middle. The earth shook, mountains trembled, and tombs opened up.

People who saw were so afraid. "He surely was the Son of God!" they said.

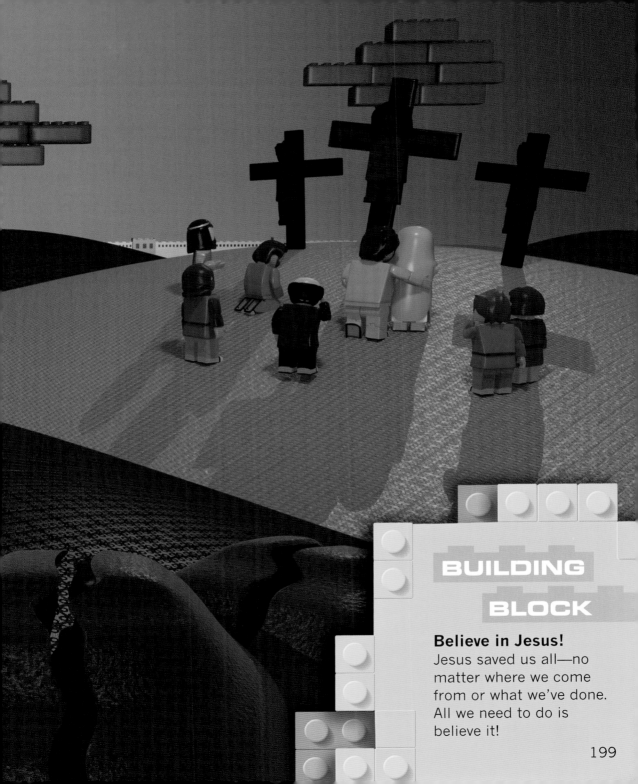

BUILDING BLOCK

Believe in Jesus!

Jesus saved us all—no matter where we come from or what we've done. All we need to do is believe it!

Jesus and the Tomb

John 20:1–18

After Jesus died, his body was wrapped in cloths and placed in a tomb. A large stone was rolled in front of the opening to seal it up.

Three days later, Mary Magdalene went to the tomb. What she saw was so amazing, she almost didn't believe her eyes. The stone in front of the tomb had been moved away, and Jesus was not inside.

She ran back to the disciples. "They have taken our Lord! He is gone!"

Peter and some other disciples went to see what she was talking about. When they arrived at the tomb, Jesus really was gone.

Peter went into the tomb. He found the strips of cloth Jesus had been wrapped in lying on the ground. But none of them understood what was going on. The disciples and Mary thought that Jesus' body had been taken.

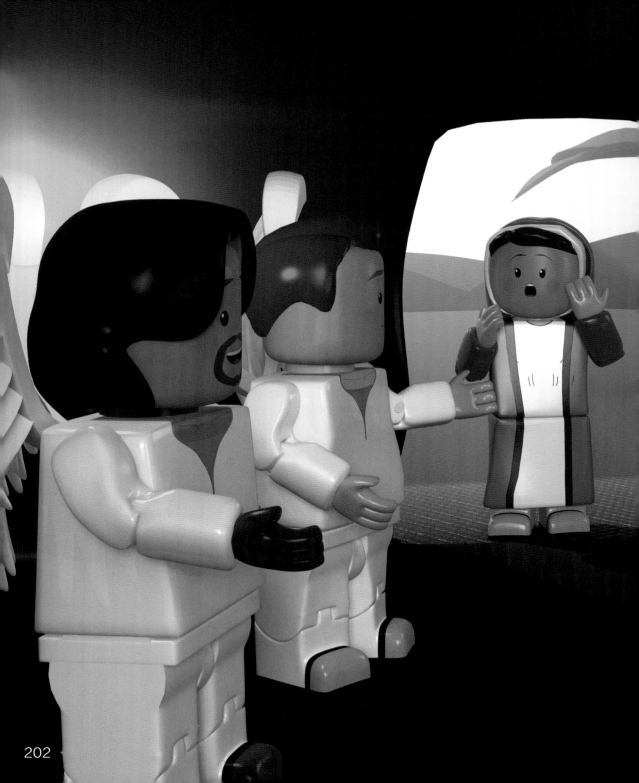

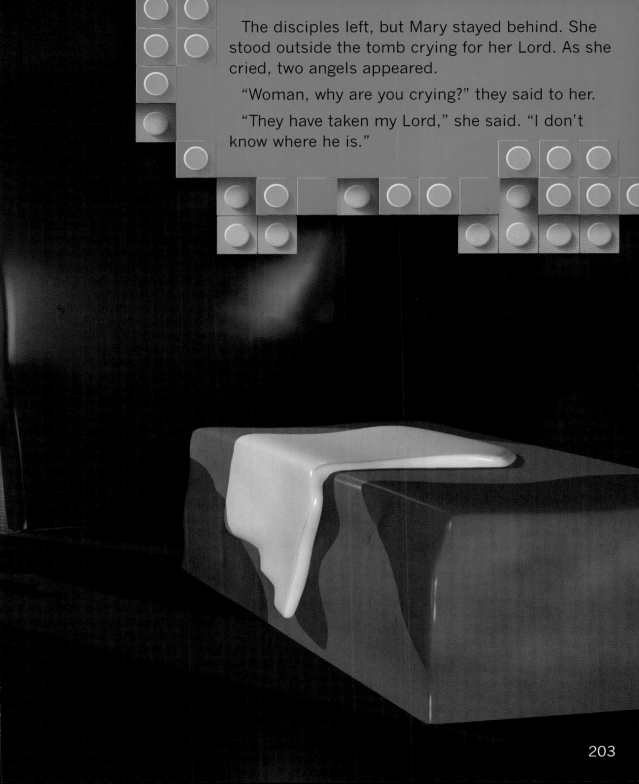

The disciples left, but Mary stayed behind. She stood outside the tomb crying for her Lord. As she cried, two angels appeared.

"Woman, why are you crying?" they said to her.

"They have taken my Lord," she said. "I don't know where he is."

As she turned around to leave, a man was standing in front of her.

"Sir, tell me where you put my Lord. I will go and get him," she said.

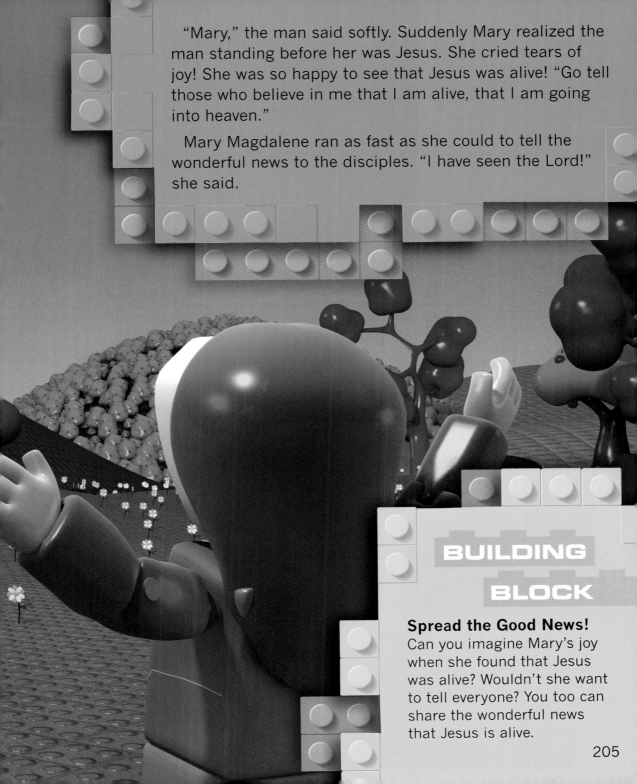

"Mary," the man said softly. Suddenly Mary realized the man standing before her was Jesus. She cried tears of joy! She was so happy to see that Jesus was alive! "Go tell those who believe in me that I am alive, that I am going into heaven."

Mary Magdalene ran as fast as she could to tell the wonderful news to the disciples. "I have seen the Lord!" she said.

BUILDING BLOCK

Spread the Good News!
Can you imagine Mary's joy when she found that Jesus was alive? Wouldn't she want to tell everyone? You too can share the wonderful news that Jesus is alive.

Jesus Appears to His Disciples

John 20:19-29   Acts 1:1-11

The disciples huddled together in the upper room. All the doors to the house had been locked so no one could get in. But the disciples were afraid. Would they get in trouble for following Jesus?

Suddenly, someone appeared before them. It was a man who looked just like Jesus! "May peace be with you," he greeted them. But the disciples didn't believe that the man standing in front of them could really be Jesus. He had died on the cross. They had all seen it!

Jesus held out his hands. The disciples stared in surprise at the holes where he had been nailed to the cross. It really was Jesus! The disciples were so happy to see him they shouted with joy!

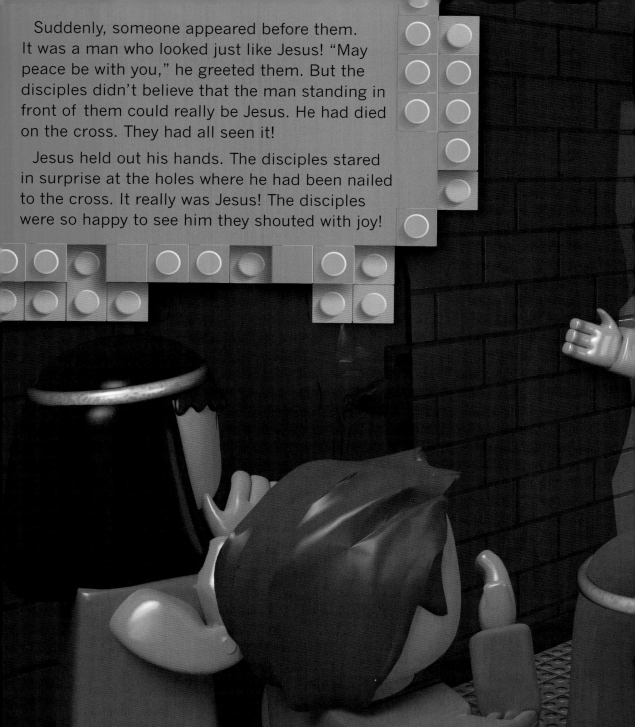

"God has sent me, so now I am sending you," Jesus told his friends. It was now the disciples' turn to spread good news and joy to others. "Receive the Holy Spirit," said Jesus. "If you forgive anyone's sins, their sins are forgiven."

The disciples looked at each other in awe. Jesus was back from the dead. Surely he was God's one true son.

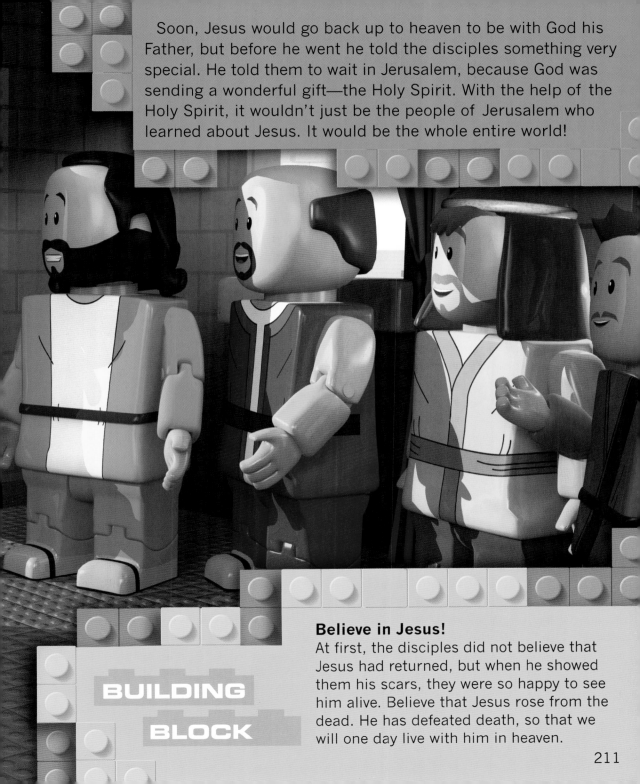

Soon, Jesus would go back up to heaven to be with God his Father, but before he went he told the disciples something very special. He told them to wait in Jerusalem, because God was sending a wonderful gift—the Holy Spirit. With the help of the Holy Spirit, it wouldn't just be the people of Jerusalem who learned about Jesus. It would be the whole entire world!

BUILDING BLOCK

Believe in Jesus!
At first, the disciples did not believe that Jesus had returned, but when he showed them his scars, they were so happy to see him alive. Believe that Jesus rose from the dead. He has defeated death, so that we will one day live with him in heaven.

The Disciples are Filled with the Holy Spirit

Acts 2:1–13

Jesus' disciples and followers came together, prayed, and waited, just as Jesus had told them to do. Suddenly a rushing sound came from the sky. It filled every corner and every space of the room where they had gathered. Above them, flickering tongues of flames rested above each head and lit up the room.

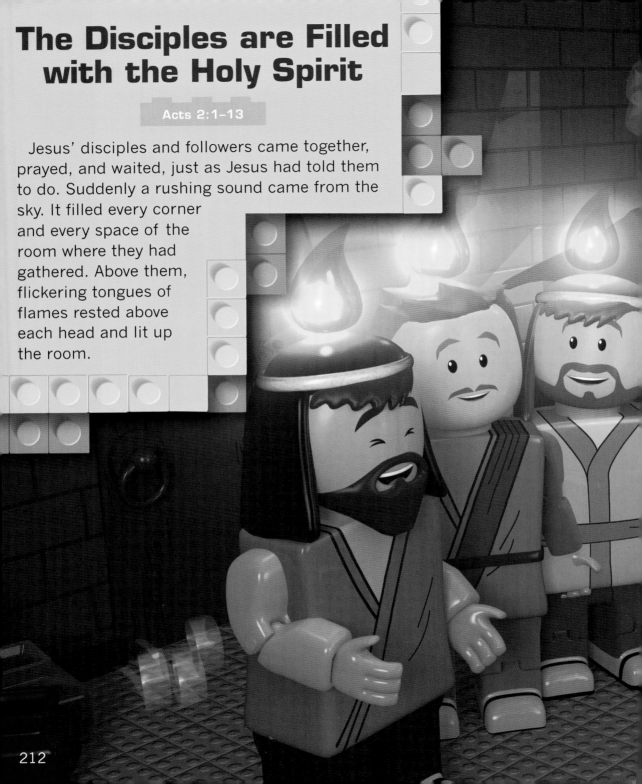

Everyone was filled with the magnificent presence of the
Holy Spirit. They began to speak in languages they didn't
know. The Holy Spirit gave them this ability so they could
go to different places to share the good news of Jesus.

People who saw and heard the disciples that day were confused. They thought they had been drinking too much wine. But the truth was the Holy Spirit had given the disciples the ability to go out and share the good news of eternal life with everyone.

Spread the Good News!
The disciples were filled with the Holy Spirit, and they were able to speak any language in order to share the good news with everyone! We need to share this good news with everyone too.

BUILDING BLOCK

217

Jesus Is Coming Back!

Revelation 21–22

Many years after Jesus returned to heaven, he showed himself to the disciple John in a vision. In the vision, he showed John the most wonderful places of all.

There was a new heaven and a new earth. John saw God there, and around God was the most beautiful rainbow. A golden gate that sparkled in the light was open to the new heaven and earth.

And one of the most brilliant things about the new heaven and earth is that everything painful and bad about the earth we live in now will be gone. There will be no more pain, no more sadness, no more crying, no more fear.

And the most magnificent thing about it all is that Jesus is going to come back to bring us there.

"I am coming back soon," Jesus said. What a perfect thing to look forward to!

222

BUILDING BLOCK

Believe in Jesus!
Jesus is building a
wonderful home for us in
heaven! He will return, and
there will be a new heaven
and earth for those who
believe in Jesus!

223